MANAGING ANGER

Methods for a Happier and Healthier Life

Rebecca R. Luhn, Ph.D.

A FIFTY-MINUTE™ SERIES BOOK

CRISP PUBLICATIONS, INC.
Menlo Park, California

MANAGING ANGER
Methods for a Happier and Healthier Life

Rebecca R. Luhn, Ph.D.

CREDITS:
Editor: **Elaine Brett**
Designer: **Carol Harris**
Typesetting: **ExecuStaff**
Cover Design: **Carol Harris**
Artwork: **Ralph Mapson**

Copyright ©1992 Crisp Publications, Inc.
Printed in the United States of America

English language Crisp books are distributed worldwide. Our major international distributors include:

CANADA: Reid Publishing Ltd., Box 69559—109 Thomas St., Oakville, Ontario, Canada L6J 7R4. TEL: (905) 842-4428, FAX: (905) 842-9327

Raincoast Books Distribution Ltd., 112 East 3rd Avenue, Vancouver, British Columbia, Canada V5T 1C8. TEL: (604) 873-6581, FAX: (604) 874-2711

AUSTRALIA: Career Builders, P.O. Box 1051, Springwood, Brisbane, Queensland, Australia 4127. TEL: 841-1061, FAX: 841-1580

NEW ZEALAND: Career Builders, P.O. Box 571, Manurewa, Auckland, New Zealand. TEL: 266-5276, FAX: 266-4152

JAPAN: Phoenix Associates Co., Mizuho Bldg. 2-12-2, Kami Osaki, Shinagawa-Ku, Tokyo 141, Japan. TEL: 3-443-7231, FAX: 3-443-7640

Selected Crisp titles are also available in other languages. Contact International Rights Manager Suzanne Kelly at (415) 323-6100 for more information.

This book is printed on recyclable paper with soy ink.

Library of Congress Catalog Card Number 91-76242
Luhn, Rebecca R.
Managing Anger
ISBN 1-56052-114-7

PREFACE

If you suffer from anger of any kind, you are in pain more than you need to be. It has been established that if anger is handled incorrectly, or not at all, it can cause cardiovascular disease, headaches, depression, relationship abuse, poor self-esteem, addictions, and other diseases.

The purpose of this book is to stop the pain and convert the negative into a positive. It is an individual assessment of the cause and effects of our anger with methods that will help us manage our emotions on a daily basis and deal with anger in a positive manner. It will help you change behavior so that you can manage your own anger and deal with the anger of others.

This book is action-oriented, with concrete activities designed to create change and give you more control over the emotion anger. It will help you find the cause of your anger, and it presents solutions that use proper and effective communication. When you master these techniques, you will be more productive in all aspects of your life. With practice, you can change your old anger habits into new positive alternatives in your personal and working relationships.

Rebecca Luhn

CONTENTS

Managing Anger

SECTION VII   REVIEW

S E C T I O N

I

What Is Anger?

HOW DOES ANGER WORK?

Anger involves complex feelings. It is made up of different reactions that cause us to be irritated, annoyed, furious, frustrated, enraged and even hurt.

Our response to anger involves our body, our behaviors and our thought process. The events that cause us to feel angry have no emotional value in themselves—it is how we appraise these events that causes a shift in our physiological arousal. It is the way we view the provocation that causes us to respond in a certain way. The event does not have to be negative to cause anger. There are many reasons why each of us responds differently to the events in our lives.

It is important to have some understanding of why we respond the way we do, but it is more important to manage our response—to manage our anger. Here is the typical sequence of events when anger occurs:

1. Anger is triggered by an event, a provocation.

2. Anger thoughts are developed.

3. The next behaviors are based on the angry thoughts.

4. Anger is fed and increases. If not managed, feelings of anger intensify and become far more difficult to control with productive action.

5. Anger that is not managed triggers a long, drawn-out, painful and destructive series of angry thoughts and actions.

In reality, it is our own thought process and actions that perpetuate anger—not the event or what someone else has said or done. Saying ''You made me feel this way'' is self-defeating. If you continue to blame others for your feelings, you will defeat your chances to change the way you act. Acknowledging that you create your own anger leads to the possibility of dealing with the provocation in a more constructive way. When you take full responsibility for your emotions, you can learn to manage your behavior in a new, predictable way. You will learn to shift your anger arousal and behavior into productive actions.

HOW DOES ANGER WORK? (Continued)

Cognitive therapists work on the theory that negative thinking patterns actually cause us to feel angry and negative. When we approach our provocations in a more positive and realistic way, we will experience greater control and happiness.

Anger is often the result of feeling that someone is treating you unfairly, or that someone is trying to take advantage of you, or you feel the threat of some kind of loss to yourself. These emotions can be continually unhealthy and destructive. The only way to break out of this state of mind is to recognize the connection between your thoughts and your emotions.

Everyone has angry feelings from time to time. You may have heard someone say, "I never get angry." They are really saying that they do not recognize their feelings as anger, or they may be hiding their anger.

You don't have to show rage to be angry. Most of the anger we experience is not violent or even considered out of control. It can simply be irritation or annoyance and a response to everyday problems. Nevertheless, it can be harmful to our relationships and to our health.

Anger can stay with us all our life if not managed properly. It can be carried from relationship to relationship. It can destroy and prevent happiness and productivity in our personal lives and professional dealings. Anger can be very powerful, and that very power can lead to our greatest productivity if it is well-managed. We must keep our provocations in perspective and see that we do not distort the anger situation. If we do not manage these feelings, we create a cycle of negative behavior throughout our lives.

To break the cycle, you must:

• Know what provokes you and identify your thought patterns at the time, your bodily changes and your behavior response.

• Be prepared to alter your thoughts and actions.

• Know and initiate productive ways to manage your feelings of anger.

SELF-EVALUATION

1. List a situation that made you angry and next to it write how you felt and/or how you still feel about it.

   ANGER SITUATION: _____ Thalias Tantrums _____

   _____

   HOW YOU FEEL ABOUT IT AND WHY: _Attacked/Abused by the_ _noise Frustrated & Inadequate when I cant prevent_ _or stop it Exhausted by the repetition_

   Now think about another feeling that you could choose to have, perhaps considering other ways it could be viewed.

   ANOTHER FEELING: _____

   _____

2. List the things you are aware of when you think of the anger situation: how you feel inside and how your body reacts.

   Upset Tearful Tense

   _____

   _____

3. List the actions you take when you feel or become angry.

   Try to be rational & think about what I want _to happen But then I move past. Shout_

   _____

4. List the actions that you should or could take instead of the negative actions you've taken in the past.

   Go away shut myself in my room

   _____

   _____

   +---+
   | **REMEMBER** |
   | Thoughts that affect our feelings of anger are |
   | the thoughts that direct our actions. |
   +---+

HOW DOES ANGER WORK? (Continued)

You already know that it is your own thoughts that cause your anger, that your beliefs and the assumptions you make cause your anger.

As stated earlier, it helps to understand the beliefs you have that are the foundations for your anger and the precursor for every angry outburst that you have.

We often judge the conduct of others based on our personal rules of how people should and should not act. In our inner thoughts, those who do not follow our rules are often judged as wrong. It is only natural to feel angry when we believe others to be in the wrong. We often impose our values and needs on someone who has different values and needs.

When we insist that others behave according to our rules, we are out of touch with reality in several ways:

1. Others have values that have been shaped from birth by their experience, and their perception is justified in their minds.

2. What *should* happen has nothing to do with what *will* happen. The real issue is how much this individual needs to respond in this way and what influence would change that.

3. How important is it to you to try to change your behavior and to influence another person's behavior?

PROCESS See the situation that angers you through the other person's eyes. When you feel your anger begin, ask these questions of yourself—and answer honestly.

1. What is the need compelling the person to respond this way?

2. What are the values being communicated that would cause this behavior?

3. What is the potential threat or loss that would provoke this response?

4. What are the limitations that influence behavior like this (fear, loss, time, manners, etc.)?

You won't always know a stranger's values, but there is a good chance that you can feel some of what the other person is feeling by assessing the situation.

Once again, remember that different people appraise things differently when they are confronted with conflict, so your point of view is important and so is the other person's.

> We ourselves can perceive the *same* event differently at different times for different reasons.

Anger between two people is often the result of each seeing a different mental picture. In learning to manage anger, we must also be aware of what to do for ourselves to put the fire out. The better you are at appraising anger accurately, the easier it will be to manage the situation.

In anger situations, we all have set behavioral models that make our anger harder to manage. For example, if you've seen others in your family deal with anger by yelling, there is a good chance you will handle anger situations in the same way.

SELF-EVALUATION

But before we go any further, let's look at appraising some of your most basic feelings and values.

1. What is it that you are thinking about changing in regard to your past anger thoughts?

   _____

   _____

2. Think of your past or present anger situation and define what values you had when you entered the situation that you'd now like to change.

   _____

   _____

3. What are some of your basic values today? Have they changed over the years?

   _____

   _____

4. Think of times you have felt angry and the way you acted or felt. Examine alternative behavior you could have demonstrated and the advantages to that change.

Past Responses to Anger Situations	Alternative	Advantage
_____	_____	_____
_____	_____	_____
_____	_____	_____

Do you think the outcome would have been different in each anger situation if you had handled it in a different way?

This is just the first step for getting in touch with your behavior. Be sure to note any patterns as you think back through each occurrence.

THOUGHTS THAT FUEL ANGER

See whether you're guilty of any of these common irrational thoughts while in an anger situation or prior to feeling angry:

1. "Things need to go a certain way because I want it that way and anything else is wrong."

2. "I must protect myself because others really don't care."

3. "I must avoid difficulty and this will relieve any pain."

4. "People should know better than to act the way they do; I can't understand their behavior."

5. "I must find perfect solutions to problems that I have."

6. "Things always go wrong when I try to plan."

7. "Life is unfair to good people."

8. "I must never hurt anyone or say what I feel."

9. "I must do well and not disappoint others."

10. "I must be in control or others will take advantage of me."

When you have these viewpoints for yourself and others, you place unrealistic expectations on everyone. These ideas also fuel the fire when we feel angry during an event or just in thought.

SELF-EVALUATION

Can you think of any other irrational ideas you may have?

1. _____

2. _____

3. _____

4. _____

5. _____

Have you ever seen any of the irrational thoughts that you listed reflected in others? If so, explain how it made you feel at the time.

_____

_____

_____

SELF-EVALUATION

Half the battle in managing anger is knowing when you should accept your beliefs, change them or express them—but it's the most important part of the process.

The following questions can help you decide what your appropriate next step is. Put a ✔ in front of statements you think are true for you.

_____ Have I felt angry for a long time?

_____ Am I doing something about these feelings or am I avoiding them?

_____ Are my thoughts realistic for the given situation?

_____ Will it help to express myself?

_____ Am I hurting myself and others about something that's beyond my control?

_____ Am I denying the truth about my feelings?

_____ Do the people around me often fail to live up to my expectations?

_____ Do I feel like a failure?

_____ Am I often depressed?

_____ Am I experiencing less and less confidence in my handling of the situation?

(Turn the page for an analysis of this self-evaluation.)

ANALYSIS OF SELF-EVALUATION

Analysis:

✔ **Have I felt angry for a long time?**
Sometimes we hang on to and focus on our anger for longer than we should. If you still feel angry over something that happened in your past, ask yourself, "Why?" and "Just how long do I intend to be miserable?" Set yourself free.

✔ **Am I doing something about these feelings or am I avoiding them?**
Negative behavior and thoughts can sometimes become a way of life. It is natural to feel disappointed over rejection or to grieve over a loss, but it is not healthy to carry this throughout our lives. Sadness can lead to depression and be displayed as negative anger in most of our thoughts.

✔ **Are my feelings realistic for the given situation?**
There are healthy negative feelings. It is best to express these as constructively as possible, to be honest and not to distort the situation. In a later section, we will discuss the differences between negative feelings that should be expressed and those that it would be damaging to express.

✔ **Will it help to express myself?**
Expressing yourself can work for you. When you are angry, you might say, "I have every right to feel as I do!" Yes, you do have the *right* to feel that way, but it may be better to change your feelings if you find you can't deal with the situation constructively.

✔ **Am I hurting myself and others about something that's beyond my control?**
If we refuse to accept situations that are beyond our control, we just cause ourselves additional anger, stress and aggravation. You do have other options if you just stop and think about it.

✔ **Am I denying the truth about my feelings?**
Sometimes one emotion can lead to another. You may be angry but you don't admit it. You find yourself repressing your feelings and end up with anxiety. This can come from a belief that you mustn't talk about problems or show that you're upset. Communicating and learning to open up can make the difference.

✔ **Do the people around me often fail to live up to my expectations?**
If you often believe that life should or must be the way you want it to be, there is a good chance that you will be angry or frustrated a great deal of the time. This can only be viewed as healthy when we take it as a signal for creativity and change.

Analysis (Continued):

✔ **Do I feel like a failure?**
Sometimes we are hard on ourselves because we think we're not as successful or as good as we should be. This leads to anger thoughts that can be reflected in relationships. Your "shoulds" can cause you distress from childhood on. You may even refuse to accept your anger and think that you *should never* fight or argue. You may fear expressing yourself because you "should know better," or you fear hurting another's feelings. Keeping things bottled up can result in constant bickering or insults. Fearing anger causes internal bitterness and conflict in most relationships. Learning to accept anger feelings and to manage them is the healthier way of living.

✔ **Am I often depressed?**
If you don't manage your anger, there is a good chance that you will become depressed. These feelings are usually based on a distorted belief about life and the future. You may even believe that you can't manage your feelings.

✔ **Am I experiencing less and less confidence in my handling of the situation?**
People with low self-esteem often have unhealthy anger. If you feel good about yourself and someone has treated you badly, you are more likely to resolve the anger constructively. If you feel inferior, you are more apt to expect rejection and to assess the situation as unfair treatment. You may take your anger out on people who have nothing to do with the situation that upset you. It is important not to berate yourself for not living up to your own expectations. Assume responsibility for your actions and you will have a more productive and joyous life.

Now it's time to look at how you cope with certain situations—situations that can breed anger thoughts and lead to anger actions.

COPING SKILLS

HOW DO YOU COPE WITH YOUR ANGER?

Each of the statements below corresponds to common coping methods. Circle the number that most closely corresponds to how frequently you act that way in difficult situations. Then total your scores for each section.

I. Withdrawal

	Often	Sometimes	Rarely	Never
1. I go to sleep when things get bad.	3	2	1	0
2. I don't get involved in problems.	3	2	1	0
3. I forget important facts.	3	2	1	0
4. I do anything to avoid facing major tasks.	3	2	1	0
5. I never get mentally into what I have to do.	3	2	1	0
6. I don't plan ahead.	3	2	1	0
7. I forget about difficult things I have to face.	3	2	1	0
8. I am cautious and shy away from risks.	3	2	1	0
9. I avoid challenges.	3	2	1	0
TOTAL:	____	____	____	____

II. Internalizing

	Often	Sometimes	Rarely	Never
1. I never like to express my feelings.	3	2	1	0
2. When I'm upset, I tend to keep it in.	3	2	1	0
3. I get frustrated.	3	2	1	0
4. I go off alone when I get upset.	3	2	1	0
5. I try not to argue even if I feel that I want to.	3	2	1	0
6. I prepare myself for pressure and pain.	3	2	1	0
TOTAL:	____	____	____	____

III. Outbursts

	Often	Sometimes	Rarely	Never
1. I often blame others for my problems.	3	2	1	0
2. I blow up.	3	2	1	0
3. I feel irritable.	3	2	1	0
4. I cry if I lose control.	3	2	1	0
5. I know when I feel angry.	3	2	1	0
TOTAL:	_____	_____	_____	_____

IV. Control

	Often	Sometimes	Rarely	Never
1. I can't do one thing without thinking of two or more I should be doing.	3	2	1	0
2. I don't recognize my achievements.	3	2	1	0
3. I put others before myself.	3	2	1	0
4. I rarely have time for myself.	3	2	1	0
5. I worry about things.	3	2	1	0
6. I don't have time for hobbies.	3	2	1	0
7. I like to do everything myself.	3	2	1	0
8. I feel impatient if I have to wait.	3	2	1	0
9. I'm rushed on most things.	3	2	1	0
10. I try to be on time for everything.	3	2	1	0
TOTAL:	_____	_____	_____	_____

INTERPRETING YOUR PROFILE

I. Withdrawal

If your score was high on **Withdrawal,** you are not meeting your responsibilities and you are holding back from life. This can lead to worry, anger and frustration.

Things to do to change:

1. Visualize yourself completing what you want done and feel the benefits.

2. Give yourself rewards for things you complete. A good feeling can defuse the hidden anger and frustration.

3. Take small steps toward expressing yourself.

4. Make a list of things you need and want to do. Also list your fears, but include the rewards for overcoming the fear.

5. Think of how you felt the last time you didn't do what you needed to do (the anger, frustration). Then think of all the reasons you don't want to feel this way again and get started.

II. Internalizing

If you scored high on **Internalizing,** you are not only building resentment and anger, but you are probably causing yourself a great deal of internal stress in an attempt to relieve the pressure.

Things to do to change:

1. Write down some reasons that you think you should not share your feelings.

2. Separate feelings from demands you're making on yourself.

3. Understand that you can express yourself without anyone else being obligated to do something about it.

4. Don't speculate about what others will think.

III. Outbursts

If you scored high on **Outbursts,** this may be the outcome of internalizing your feelings of helplessness. Shifting blame and responsibility for outbursts is a self-defeating response to anger. This is passing on the anger to another, not addressing the problem.

Things to do to change:

1. Become aware of the emotions that trigger the outbursts.

2. Ask yourself why you feel the way you do.

3. Ask yourself if there is a better way to express yourself.

IV. Control

If you scored high on **Control,** your behavior is probably Type A—you try to control every situation and to plan for every possible problem. Keeping control over one's world becomes too much and creates anger and anxiety. We become tired and frustrated taking care of everything around us.

Things to do to change:

1. Evaluate all priorities and tasks.

2. Confront the fear of not being in control.

3. Look honestly at the beliefs and feelings that are behind your behavior.

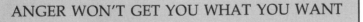

ANGER WON'T GET YOU WHAT YOU WANT

CHANGING COPING TECHNIQUES

It is not easy to change a long-standing belief or behavior. But if it is causing you or others pain, it is necessary. We will look at techniques that can work for you in the coming chapters.

Let's begin with a short *honesty* exercise:

In the space below, write out a complete description of a relationship that is very important to you—someone you care for but with whom you feel frustration and anger. Write out everything you can think of to describe the way you view that person: values, beliefs, habits and so on.

Read over your description and be honest in your assessment. Ask yourself which items are really judgments.

Now go back over your list and rewrite the judgments you found using a more neutral description.

    Example: Instead of saying ''She is short,'' say ''She is five feet tall.''

Does the description seem more accurate to you when it is nonjudgmental?

Honesty Exercise

Description: _____

_____

_____

_____

_____

_____

_____

New Description: _____

_____

_____

_____

_____

_____

_____

_____

REWRITE YOUR JUDGMENTS

OLD ANGER FEELINGS

Feelings When Anger Is Not Managed

- Suspicion
- Frustration
- Discouragement
- Fear
- Disappointment
- Guilt
- Hostility
- Jealousy
- Loneliness
- Inferiority
- Rejection
- Inadequacy
- Envy
- Impatience
- Boredom

HOW YOU WOULD RATHER FEEL

Feelings When Anger Is Managed	Characteristics When Anger Is Managed	Managed Anger Offers
Understanding	Sincere	Growth
Confidence	Relaxed	Success
Hope	Courteous	Love
Fortitude	Happy	Energy
Support	Motivated	Security
Reality	Optimistic	Health
Belief	Considerate	Self-Esteem
	Trusting	Satisfaction
		Pride

Keep this list handy and the next time you have an anger encounter, pick out the feelings you have and write down how you'd rather feel.

"No man is angry that feels not himself hurt."
Francis Bacon, Essays, "Of Anger" (1625)

SELF-EVALUATION

The last exercise in this section will help you with the process of self-analysis. You will begin to define some of your beliefs, weaknesses and strengths.

In order to manage anger, you must identify your anger, past, present and even future.

Please answer the following:

1. It is often the things you criticize in others that are the very things the other person needs help with from you. What are some of the criticisms you have of people you know? Spouse? Children? Co-workers? Friends?

_____

_____

_____

_____

_____

_____

_____

_____

_____

2. What are some weaknesses (not faults) of people you care for?

_____

_____

_____

_____

_____

_____

_____

_____

_____

3. Describe in detail a situation that resulted in someone treating you unjustly, rudely or in a hurtful way. Did you feel angry? Do you still feel angry just thinking about it?

_____

_____

_____

_____

4. Can you recall making the situation worse when you fought back, argued or became hostile? Describe what happened:

_____

_____

_____

_____

5. Have you used any technique in the past to help calm your inner thoughts or your outbursts? What worked?

_____

_____

_____

_____

6. Do you put off communicating about problems? Is there one that you're keeping inside now? Please write it out if there is.

_____

_____

_____

_____

_____

_____

A CLOSER LOOK AT NEGATIVE THINKING

You should now have a clearer understanding of your anger thoughts. In this section we will look at what actually provokes you and at the problems that your anger may present for you and others.

Remember that your thoughts and your feelings are interconnected. So before we continue, it is important to understand the forms of negative thinking that can be a precursor to your anger. You already know that specific kinds of negative thoughts cause negative behavior. Not all negative thoughts are bad or lead to anger situations, but when they are distorted and unrealistic, they powerfully affect your mood, even though they seem absolutely valid at the time.

Profiles of Negative Thinking

Exaggeration	You magnify the importance of problems or you minimize the good things in your life.
Mind Reading	You jump to conclusions and interpret things negatively. You often predict that something bad will happen and conclude that someone is against you.
Black or White	You have an all-or-nothing attitude. If a project does not turn out perfectly, you see it as a total failure.
Dwelling	You pick out a negative situation and think about it exclusively so that reality is dark and hopeless. One criticism can ruin many positive statements. You obsess about the little negative things and ignore the positive.
Discounting	You discount the positive and never give yourself or others credit for a job well done. Often you say that "It wasn't good enough," or "It could have been better." Because you then feel unrewarded you build anger.
Expectations	You tell yourself that things should be a certain way, that people should act a certain way. This leads to anger and frustration with yourself and others.

Labels   The all-or-nothing syndrome. You may label yourself as a fool or a loser or stupid. You may also label others: "He's a jerk." You'll end up with many negative interpretations and hopelessness for the future. Communication usually stops in your caring relationships when you apply such labels.

Blaming   You want and need control. If an event goes wrong, you may blame yourself, even if you are not responsible. Some people blame others for all their problems and reject responsibility. Either way, it doesn't work well. It adds resentment to relationships and fuels internal anger.

Refer to these profiles of negative thoughts as you go through the exercises in this book. Once again, remember negative thoughts are sometimes healthy and appropriate—even anger.

Don't be conned by misery!
It's often best to admit and accept negative feelings.

IDENTIFYING DISTORTED THOUGHTS

Now review the anger situations that you wrote down in this section. See if you can identify any of the misuses of thoughts that are related to anger feelings. Look for:

- *Should statements,* such as "You shouldn't have been so fast to act!"

- *Blaming,* such as "She never cares for others, and this couldn't have happened if she did."

- *Labeling,* such as "He's a jerk!"

- *Expectations,* such as "I could have done it better."

Write down distortions you may have or have had in the past:

1. _____

2. _____

3. _____

4. _____

5. _____

CONGRATULATIONS! You're ready for your journey of change and management. You have collected thoughts and tools for successfully managing your anger. Now you will apply what you've discovered about yourself so far. The next sections will take you on a growth journey through a vital aspect of your emotions. You will first look at the experience of being human and begin to understand your anger. The more you are in touch with your anger provocations, the more you are in touch with your life. Since feelings pulsate through all areas of relationships, it's an appropriate place to begin.

For many of us, feelings are friends and we use them to connect with others and grow in life. Some of us listen to what we're feeling and respond appropriately. These people are skillful in working with emotions. You can be skillful, too, even if in the past you've displayed little understanding of your anger. You can learn to be comfortable with this feeling and with other emotions. There are many reasons for discomfort. You may not know how to connect, or so many feelings are locked up inside that when you *do* communicate, it comes out in destructive ways. Obviously, these are not the ways you would choose to deal with your feelings of anger.

ANGER MANAGEMENT

To work skillfully on anger management, make these commitments about how you will do the exercises in this book:

1. Feel and be honest about the feelings. Express yourself openly.

- Try to be open to your feelings.
- Learn how to listen.
- Find creative ways of expressing yourself.
- Experiment to discover healthy outlets for anger energy.
- Express your emotions—don't indulge them.

2. Work at changing your negative beliefs that are causing your upsets.

- Our beliefs are the root of our emotion; understand what your beliefs are and why you have them.
- Changing requires a real commitment.
- Without control over your beliefs, you may feel powerless.
- You can replace old beliefs with new beliefs through self-examination.
- Create a visualization for the change.
- Rehearse your new techniques.

3. Let go of the past and clear the way for a positive future.

- Release the hurt for peace of mind.
- Letting go requires inner strength and courage.
- Use "paused" energy to create a new you.
- When memory brings pain, take time to review the release process.

Some of these suggestions—such as "paused" energy—may be new to you. We will go into more detail in Section II.

SECTION

II

The Way You Feel

"Nothing on Earth consumes a man more quickly
than the passion of resentment."

Nietzsche, Ecce Homo (1881)

WHAT PROVOKES YOU?

It is important to know why you get angry and to understand what actually provokes you. Here is what's possible when you have this clarity:

1. You can create techniques in advance for managing the provocation the next time you are faced with it. This helps to stop the full escalation of anger.

2. You learn how to avoid certain situations that trigger anger, and in most cases you can prevent anger thoughts.

3. When you know what provokes you, you can practice management skills that will build up your tolerance for anger situations.

4. If you know what triggers your anger, you can stop the gun from going off.

When your thoughts are free of distortions, it becomes easier to break the anger cycle. You become more productive and channel your energy in a positive and constructive way.

Most of what makes us angry can be classified in the following ways:

Injustice—These occurrences make you feel that you have been treated unfairly. It may be a time when you are accused of doing something wrong and blamed without any proof or justification.

Hurt—We get angry when we've been hurt or abused verbally or physically. Statements, name calling and unkind words often cause lasting pain. Hitting, punching or physical pain can scar also.

Frustration—It is not uncommon to hear people say "I'm frustrated" when the truth is that they are angry, and their feelings have long passed the stage of frustration. We often first become frustrated when we cannot get something done our way or we're disappointed. This can lead to aggressive behavior that has not been worked out in a constructive manner.

Annoyances—Life's little irritations get on our nerves; when they begin stacking up, they leave us feeling out of control. A traffic jam is a good example; it can be irritating at first and then lead to anger as other annoyances happen.

You are the one who has to appraise each situation and decide whether an occurrence is unfair, abusive, frustrating or annoying. Knowing where your provocations fall in these classifications can help you learn lasting skills to manage your behavior.

WHAT PROVOKES YOU? (Continued)

Remember that you are trying to identify what provokes you, not what provokes someone else. Things that cause anger thoughts for you may not trouble someone else at all.

Yes, there are areas of provocation common to most of us:

- Money problems
- Conflict with a boss
- Family arguments
- Irresponsibility
- Rudeness

If the first few techniques you try don't work in an anger situation, *don't give up!* Keep trying alternatives until one works for you. Give each try enough time, and with each day, you'll improve. This doesn't mean that if you see something working for someone else, you can't try it. Your techniques do not have to be original.

If you know someone who is a good role model in the way they manage anger, try his or her technique. If it doesn't feel right, modify it. If it still doesn't work, find another model. Sometimes it is easier to create your own model in your mind. By defining and practicing the way you want to be, it is easier to face the situation in real life.

VISUALIZATION EXERCISE

1. Recall a moderate provocation you've had.

2. Close your eyes and make sure you have a clear picture of the scene. Use all your senses.

3. Hold the image and feel any changes in your body (tension, heart rate).

4. Now take a deep breath and relax your muscles. Breathe in and out very slowly.

5. Keep your provocation in mind and picture your anger and feel your anger.

6. Repeat step #4. RELAX.

7. Repeat steps #4 and #5 until your provocation becomes less important to you and you manage the feelings easily with relaxation.

Note: Do this with several provoking situations you can recall until you can recognize all the signs of anger in your mind and body. Write them out when you identify them.

Example: I felt my pulse accelerate.   I felt my head hurt.

   I felt my mouth become dry.   I felt my heart race.

VISUALIZATION IS POWERFUL
- Use it to manage feelings.   • Use it to focus on the life you want.

AN OUNCE OF PREVENTION

Knowing what your provocations are also enables you to use preventative strategies. You *are not* running away from the problem, but using constructive creativity while bypassing the anger.

How do you do this?

1. Write down a provocation.

2. List constructive ways to manage the situation without confrontation.

This will take some work each time you feel anger thoughts, but it is well worth it once you develop skills that will become new and spontaneous.

This is more than "anger management"—this is mood therapy and charting your own destiny!

SELF-EVALUATION

1. Allow yourself some time to consider your most intense anger situations. List them according to how much of a problem they are and how severely you respond, note any misconceptions or wrong beliefs you may have. Next to each, write out something you can do to manage your behavior for each situation the next time this anger happens.

	Intense Provocation	*Incorrect Belief*	*Management Technique*
1.			
2.			
3.			
4.			
5.			

2. Use visualization for each provocation.

3. Develop your preventative strategy for each provocation.

   Anger Situation #1: _____

   _____

   _____

   Preventative Technique: _____

   _____

   _____

   Anger Situation #2: _____

   _____

   _____

   Preventative Technique: _____

   _____

   _____

Anger Situation #3: _____

_____

_____

Preventative Technique: _____

_____

_____

Anger Situation #4: _____

_____

_____

Preventative Technique: _____

_____

_____

Anger Situation #5: _____

_____

_____

Preventative Technique: _____

_____

_____

Note: There are times when your anger response is not because of a belief. You are just angry. We will discuss this in another chapter.

HONESTY NOTES The space below is provided for any ''honesty notes'' you may want to make to yourself—things you want to remember about your feelings or visualization exercises you've just completed. Use it as a journal that you can refer to often.

WHAT PROVOKES YOU? (Continued)

STAYING *ALIVE*

ALIVE is a useful acronym for five steps that can lead to a more constructive approach to anger situations.

A = Accept your problem.

L = List your response.

I = Identify alternatives.

V = Visualize your situation.

E = Evaluate the conclusion.

Accept your problem. Don't run away from your anger or internalize it. Know where your problems are.

List your response. Describe how you usually respond in tough situations. Be specific. Use all the facts.

Identify alternatives. Generate constructive solutions.

Visualize your situation. Remember the rules of visualization and practice your coping techniques.

Evaluate the conclusion. Determine what works and whether you really obtained the outcome you want for a happier, healthier life. Are you getting long-term benefits?

Problems are a part of life. Learn how to manage your responses and you'll stay ALIVE with goals and loving relationships.

PROBLEMS, PROBLEMS, PROBLEMS

On the Job and in Relationships

Anger does not work any better on the job than it does with family or friends. It is all too common for the Type-A personality to reach a stage of burnout. The outcome is the same for most: withdrawal, attacks, counterattacks, defensiveness and even paranoia. Those who do not manage anger in the office usually end up moving from department to department and job to job. They are less productive, unmotivated and often jealous of others. They place blame on others and quite often feed into office gossip. They take their frustration out on employees and co-workers and then carry it home.

Relationships become more defensive and distant. There seem to be fewer and fewer opportunities, and the highest price of all is isolation. Cynical attitudes toward others result in loneliness.

How much of a problem? Too much when . . .

- You are angry too often.
- It is too strong of a feeling.
- It leads to aggressive behavior.
- It rules your life.

Most angry people keep others at bay or drive them away. Low self-esteem is a factor, and life loses its meaning.

SELF-EVALUATION

Now is the time to go beyond honesty with yourself. What is the real cost of your anger?

Impact Scale: 0 = No impact; 1 = Minor problems; 2 = Some problems;

3 = Many problems; 4= Always a problem

Use the scale above to rate the impact of your anger on the following:

1. Communicating with co-workers and the boss _____
2. Communicating with other departments at the office _____
3. Communicating with clients and business associates outside of the office _____
4. Communicating with your spouse _____
5. Communicating with your children _____
6. Communicating with your parents _____
7. Contact with neighbors _____
8. Contact with organizations or associations _____
9. Impact on health _____
10. Impact on relaxation _____
11. Use of drugs or alcohol _____
12. Mistakes and errors _____
13. Wanted relationships _____
14. Time lost _____
15. Impact on having fun and social events _____
16. Impact on daily activities (driving a car, reading, etc.) _____

Take a close look at areas of your life that are most affected by your anger. Now list the things you can think of that are not on the list above.

1. _____
2. _____
3. _____
4. _____
5. _____

WHEN TO BE ANGRY

As you have learned, anger can escalate and lead to destructive statements and actions. When you lash out physically or verbally, you let your anger control you and your life situations. When your anger is hot, it is difficult to put it on the back burner and deal with it at a later time. But there are times when you need to call time-out and forget the feeling. Many of those times are exactly the situations that cost you the most when you express your anger.

There are times when dealing with anger, even in a constructive way, is not appropriate. There are situations such as a staff meeting, a client meeting and in relationship conflicts when you know the other person is not prepared to be reasonable. You've heard the saying, "Timing is everything." Well, this holds true for anger management. Be creative and practice mental time-outs even if you cannot physically leave the room at the time. Mentally tell yourself, "I'm beginning to feel angry and I want to take a time-out!" Take a deep breath and give yourself positive self-statements. Stay calm, and later think out your situation and decide how you'll address it in a constructive manner.

If you can physically remove yourself for a period of time, do so. This gives your body time to cool down and relax. This is not the time to think about the anger situation. This is time to relax and discharge some of your anger by doing something else. Take a walk, jog, read, clean something or watch television. Don't use drugs, call a friend to talk about the problem.

Some situations are too volatile to deal with even after a short break. Take as long as you need until you have confidence that you can handle and manage the situation in a productive way.

In the past few exercises, you've been given the opportunity to assess several of your provocations and anger situations. But do you have a good understanding of what is happening when you feel angry?

At this stage of the anger management process, you should have answers to the following questions. If you are not yet comfortable with your responses, go back and repeat the exercise in this section and in Section I.

SELF-EVALUATION

SELF-EVALUATION

1. What are my "hot buttons"—the situations that cause anger thoughts and provocations? _____

_____

_____

_____

2. What old feelings are triggered when a button is pushed? What is my usual behavior response? _____

_____

_____

_____

3. What are the core beliefs behind my response? _____

_____

_____

_____

4. How would I like to react and feel? What can I do to change my behavior?

_____

_____

_____

_____

5. What are some techniques that work for me before I become emotionally out of control? _____

_____

_____

_____

6. How does visualization work for me? At what point will I find it useful?

_____

_____

_____

_____

YOUR BODY AND ANGER

Your body gives you signals to tell you how it feels when you become angry. If you fail to listen to your body, you can risk serious health problems.

Tension is the first stage in the anger process. When your muscles tighten and you get headaches or chest tension, you should recognize that tension is high. Tension is the residue that is left when you can't do something about your problems. Over time, tension lets you know that you're wearing down, and illness in the form of physical or emotional breakdown is the final result.

Anger escalation brings on physical effects such as increased blood glucose, heart rate and blood pressure; shallow, difficult breathing; back and head pain; and sweating. These are just a few of the signals of body stress that can lead to chronic illness.

The mental effects of anger are difficulty in concentrating, poor performance, sleeplessness and lack of focus. These can lead to other emotional problems such as depression, fatigue, irritability, nervousness and worry.

The behavioral effects of anger can be drug use, overeating, alcoholism, smoking, restlessness, impulsiveness, compulsiveness, withdrawal and isolation.

The organizational effects of chronic anger are job burnout, dissatisfaction, lawsuits, poor relationships, job turnover and accidents. The figure below charts the cycle of problems leading to anger, leading to problems, and so on.

The Pain

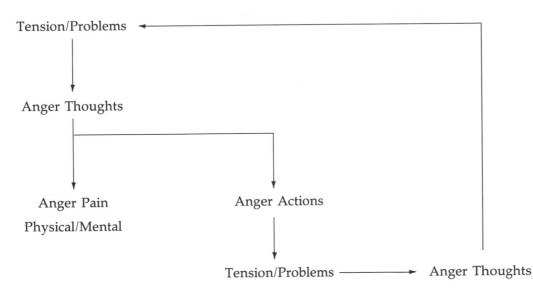

YOUR BODY AND ANGER (Continued)

HYPERTENSION

To understand the relationship between anger and high blood pressure, it is important to know a little about how the vascular system—the amazing system of blood vessels in the body—works.

Blood pressure readings give two results. The systolic pressure is the higher number you have and the lower is diastolic pressure.

Example: 125/85, where 125 = systolic pressure

85 = diastolic pressure

A blood pressure of 125/85 means that the pressure in the arteries is 125 at the time of the heart's contraction and 85 between beats. There is a high level of the chemical norepinephrine associated with anger, and this raises the diastolic blood pressure between beats by constricting the large peripheral blood vessels.

In studies of many emotions, anger caused the greatest increase in heart rate. There is evidence that anger thoughts contribute to the development of hypertension for many susceptible people. Additional studies have shown that anger expressed in a hostile way raises the blood pressure even more. Anything that interferes with normal coronary functions is considered life-threatening.

ANGER AND YOUR DIGESTION

Anyone who experiences anger on a regular basis knows of the impact on the stomach. The increase of hydrochloric acid can cause gastritis, ulcers and even colon problems. It is believed that the mucous membrane of the colon reacts sharply to suppressed anger.

SELF-EVALUATION

In order to manage the physical responses that anger has on your body, it is important to be in touch with understanding the present condition your body is in. Take a few deep breaths and answer the following questions. It will be a good heart-to-heart talk with your body.

1. Are you in good physical condition, and how do you feel about this?

   _____

   _____

2. Is your heart as healthy as you'd like it to be?

   _____

   _____

3. Do you eat right? Low fat, low sodium, no overeating, no days of skipping meals?

   _____

   _____

4. Do you exercise regularly?

   _____

   _____

5. Do you feel ill more often than you'd like?

   _____

   _____

6. Do you have tension headaches and tense muscles?

   _____

   _____

7. Do you get the appropriate amount of rest?

   _____

   _____

8. Do you know when and how to relax?

   _____

   _____

YOUR BODY AND ANGER (Continued)

Finally, write down any changes you would like to make in your body. Be specific and include any feelings and physical pain you believe are caused by your anger.

_____

_____

_____

_____

_____

_____

_____

_____

_____

_____

> How you want your body to be
>
> is your choice!

We will discuss relaxation techniques in another section, but for now we'll briefly discuss some things you can do to help yourself with the physical effects of anger.

Nutrition affects your anger management in several ways. You can use good nutrition to calm yourself. Here are several suggestions:

- Reduce sodium, which contributes to high blood pressure.

- Eat slowly in a quiet setting.

- Eat more complex carbohydrates to help maintain the energy that anger depletes.

- Avoid using food to suppress anger.

Exercise is useful in managing anger. You can:

- Walk when you're angry—use the energy in a positive way.

- Exercise several times a week—it keeps you in shape for the stressful times.

SECTION

III

Using Anger to Improve Your Life

ANGER: PAIN OR GAIN?

We have already talked about anger being valid, but what you must understand is that anger is an expression, a feeling that you have every right to.

LEARN TO:

- Accept and validate your anger

- Acknowledge your feelings

When you accept your anger, you move toward constructive validation of your feelings. You will no longer try to suppress or deny that you are angry. This will enable you to grow in a way that will work. Failure to do this is counterproductive for your emotional stability.

BEGIN BY SAYING:

- *"I feel angry."*
  Anger has no value if you do not grow from it in a productive, positive way. (The question below will help you know whether your anger is going to do any good.)

- *"Is being angry at this time going to help my current situation?"*
  Most of the time our anger is useless to us because of the way we use it or respond to it, not because we feel angry.

The example we used earlier about being angry over getting stuck in a traffic jam is needless anger. This is a situation in which your anger will not do you any good.

If you become angry over a job you did badly and you give up, then your anger will hurt your confidence for the future and cause yourself additional self-esteem problems.

PRACTICE THESE APPROACHES:

- Use anger to increase your drive, to try harder, to learn more!

- Use anger to develop patience and perform relaxation techniques.

THE GOOD AND BAD OF ANGER

If used correctly, anger can be good. *Good anger can:*

- Energize
- Release tension in a constructive way
- Help you communicate when you're upset
- Resolve hidden conflict
- Give you new thoughts
- Alert you to threats
- Provide information

If used inappropriately, anger produces negative results. *Negative anger can:*

- Disrupt your life
- Control your thoughts
- Ruin relationships
- Cause pain
- Cause health problems
- Cause other emotional problems
- Leave a negative impression

JUST OR UNJUST?

"Just" anger means that your anger is free of cognitive distortions; that you have a "right" to be angry under the circumstances. It means that, given the same place and time and the same situation, most other people would be angry, too.

How do you know when your anger is just? Ask yourself the following questions:

1. Is my anger the result of a real and intentional threat?

2. Am I angry with someone who has purposefully acted toward me in a hurtful manner?

If you answer yes in anger situations, then your anger is "just" to you and to most others.

"Just" Examples

- Your lover lies to you about other relationships.
- Someone sets you up in an embarrassing situation.
- You are betrayed by someone you trust.
- You are made a promise that is never kept.

"Unjust" Examples

- You get stuck in traffic.
- Someone is sick and can't make it to a meeting you planned.
- It rains on your vacation.
- The noise down the hall is too loud while you're trying to work.

We often become upset when there is no intention to harm or hurt us or someone or something we care about. We become angry because we perceive the situation as other than what it is. Your distorted view triggers your anger thoughts and brings about a negative situation.

When your anger is just, use it as a source of energy to change a negative into a situation that will help you or eliminate the threat and hurt. Acting forcefully—yelling, hitting, or seeking revenge—will only breed more anger and hostility.

Even when you know that your anger is just, you must learn how to express your anger in a rational manner. The chart on the next page will help you understand the basics of just and unjust anger.

BASICS OF JUST AND UNJUST ANGER

Legitimate	Useless	Just and Unjust
Anger is always valid. It is an emotion, a feeling you need not deny yourself.	Anger is useless when it causes you problems, or when it hurts you or others and leads to destructive behavior.	Anger can be just when there was an intent to hurt, but it must be handled constructively. Your anger is unjust when you distort and attack when there was no intent to harm you.

Remember, don't create a problem where there was none.

TAKING RESPONSIBILITY

1. Ask yourself: "Is my anger hurting me or others?"

2. Ask yourself: "Is my anger just, and how can I handle it constructively?"

3. Ask yourself: "How can I learn to make my anger work for me, not against me?"

CHECK-UP

1. How many times do you get angry (just or unjust) in a week? _____

2. Is your anger hurting you and others? _____

3. How long do you stay angry? _____

4. Does your anger lead to aggression? _____

ANGER AND YOUR COMMUNICATION STYLE

In the communication process, you may intentionally or inadvertently set up roadblocks that create problems, anger and hostility. The "right" message, the "right" way may never get through from one side to the other. Sometimes the message is delayed, creating problems and misunderstandings. Or the meaning of questions or reactions may change drastically in the process of transmission from you to the receiver.

The causes of these communication breakdowns can often be attributed to the following:

Lack of sensitivity. It can be dangerous and destructive to be unaware of others' feelings. People want to be recognized as individuals with feelings of their own.

Wrong choice. The wrong choice of words at the wrong time can send a hurtful, harmful message.

Leaping before thinking. Leaping to conclusions and making false assumptions can cause a chain of misunderstanding.

Other types of communication behavior that are almost always perceived as threatening, hostile, attacking or otherwise *angry* are:

Evaluation. Speech or other behavior that appears to be evaluative increases defensiveness on the part of the listener–observer. Most people do not like to be judged.

Control. Whenever we have the feeling that another person is trying to manipulate us or is trying to control us in some way that restrains our freedom, we tend to resist such control.

Strategy. Whenever we have the feeling that someone is playing games with us in which they have some ulterior motive, we tend to become resentful or equally cagey, or we abandon our best mode of communication and start responding with equally deceptive game playing.

Superiority. To assume that you are better than the other person will end effective communication.

Certainty. Expressing certainty in the wrong tone tends to arouse resistance in the listener.

HOW ANGRY DO YOU BECOME WHEN YOU'RE NOT LISTENED TO?

Listening is crucial to communicating effectively and reducing anger.* It says:

- I am interested in you as a person.
- I respect you as a person.
- I am not trying to evaluate you.
- I want to understand you.
- I think this relationship is worth listening to.

STYLES THAT AFFECT THE WAY WE COMMUNICATE

The style in which we communicate and relate to other people can affect our attitudes toward what happens and contribute to either anger or a constructive response. See if you can identify yourself as having one of these three styles:

PASSIVE

- You express your needs indirectly.
- You avoid conflicts.
- You find it hard to say no.
- You feel helpless.
- Your needs are not met.
- Your pain builds.
- You blame others.
- You feel invisible.
- Others have to guess what you want.

AGGRESSIVE

- You have an impulse to punish.
- People resist you.
- You have a lot of conflict.
- You want control.
- You are pushy.
- You are overwhelming.

ASSERTIVE

- You present facts.
- You reduce anger.
- You stand up for your rights.
- You look toward a settlement and solution.
- You set limits.

*For more on listening skills, order *The Business of Listening* by Diane Bone, published by Crisp Publications, Inc. See the back of the book.

EXPRESS YOURSELF EFFECTIVELY

Obviously, an assertive style is most likely to avoid conflict and to give you the satisfaction of managing your emotions effectively. Express yourself effectively by:

- Acknowledging the other person's feelings
- Stating your position with confidence
- Saying no if you mean no
- Taking your time
- Not over-apologizing
- Not putting yourself or others down
- Being specific
- Being aware of voice and body language
- Letting go of guilt
- Dealing with criticism

COMMUNICATING HABITS THAT CAN FUEL ANGER

Some communication habits are almost certain to irritate the other party and often lead to anger and conflict. Review the following lists honestly to see whether you have any of these communication habits.

Conversational Habits

- Not giving someone a chance to talk
- Interrupting while someone else is talking
- Being rushed for time
- Not looking at the other person when they talk
- Acting like the conversation is wasting your time
- Acting bored
- Pacing and showing impatience
- Keeping a poker face
- Being sarcastic
- Finishing someone's story
- Rephrasing what was said in a negative way
- Asking a question that was just asked by someone else
- Walking out of the room to take a call or talk to someone else

OTHER COMMUNICATION CLUES

Territorial Dominance

- Feet on desk
- Leaning over the desk
- Hands behind desk
- Sitting on desk or the chair arm

Nervousness

- Clearing throat
- Whistling
- Fidgeting
- Hand over your mouth while speaking
- Jingling keys or money in pockets
- Wringing your hands
- Tapping a pencil

Frustration

- Short breaths
- "Tsk" sound
- Clenched hands
- Fist-like gestures
- Running your hand through your hair
- Kicking the ground

Self-Control

- Gripping your wrists
- Locking your ankles
- Clenching your hands

Boredom

- Doodling
- Drumming
- Legs crossed
- Head in palm of hand
- Blank stare

Reassurance

- Touching
- Pinching your flesh
- Hands in your pockets

Cooperation

- Open hands
- Sitting on the edge of your chair
- Hand to face gestures
- Unbuttoning coat
- Head tilted

Openness

- Open hands
- Unbuttoned coat

Defensiveness

- Arms crossed
- Crossing legs
- Pointing index finger
- Stiff posture

Evaluation

- Hand to face gestures
- Head tilted
- Stroking chin
- Peering over glasses
- Getting up from table and walking around

Suspicion

- Not looking at you
- Arms crossed
- Moving away from you
- Sideways glance
- Rubbing eyes

Readiness

- Hands on hips
- Sitting on edge of chair
- Moving closer
- Putting coat on

Confidence

- Hands in back
- Back stiffened
- Hands on lapel of coat
- Hands in coat pockets

USE PARAPHRASING TO HELP ELIMINATE ANGER SITUATIONS

Communication is often involved in anger situations because we do not check to see whether or not we really understand what is being said. Even when the other person is expressing hurt feelings, we usually respond with ''I see'' or ''I understand'' when we really do not see or understand at all. Sometimes we are even thinking about what we will say next instead of accurately hearing the message sent.

One way to make sure you have accurately interpreted what is being communicated to you is to use the technique of **paraphrasing.** Paraphrasing is restating in your own words what you have heard someone else say. It is a way of revealing your understanding of the other person's message and finding out whether the remark means the same to you as it does to him or her.

Paraphrasing

- Lets the speaker know if you are listening and are interested
- Shows that you understand the message being communicated
- Allows you to request more information when you do not understand
- Helps the speaker clarify his or her thoughts
- Keeps the conversation on the subject
- Encourages original thought and opinions

Paraphrasing is especially helpful when

- You need to be sure you understand the other person's meaning
- The other person is overwhelmed with emotion
- You want to build a trusting relationship.

SECTION

IV

Stopping Anger from Escalating

TIPS FOR HANDLING CRITICISM

QUESTION

Properly communicated criticism can be constructive and valid. Feedback can help relationships and help you grow. When you respond to criticism by asking questions, you are better able to assess what the critic is really saying. You are less likely to become angry over something you didn't understand. Sometimes a critical statement means something other than what the words convey. At the heart of the criticism, there may be feelings that it is important for you to understand.

LESSEN THE HURT

You can limit the escalation of anger by stopping attacks from others when they are not constructive. Even if something is wrong or you've done something, you don't have to listen to abusive language. You're also hearing only one opinion about one thing you've done. Don't contribute to the attack, and don't take anything said as representing the truth about who you are and what you do. Also, you're human like everyone else and unlikely to achieve the perfection you picture in your mind. If you can accept yourself as a human being who sometimes makes mistakes, you will limit a great deal of your anger feelings and angry moments.

DISARM

You can prevent anger escalation by keeping a cool head when your critic is coming at you. Think about the words the critic is using and ask yourself whether there is any truth to the critic's representation of the problem. Listen carefully and paraphrase only what you agree with in your response to the critic.

Example:

> *Critic:* "This is your fault. If you hadn't been late, this would have never happened."
> *Response:* "Yes, I was late and I've apologized for that, but that isn't the problem now."

You can also agree in principle without agreeing with all that is said. Remember, it can help to acknowledge the criticism, but you can disagree with it.

> *Response:* "I understand that you're upset, but I don't believe I've caused the problem here."

Note: Don't blame—listen. When confronted, be assertive but not angry.

More tips are available in the book *Giving and Receiving Criticism* by Patti Hathaway. See the back of this book for more information.

RELAXATION

You can also deal with anger escalation by practicing forms of relaxation. Relaxation is extremely helpful in many situations, and it is vital to a healthy, happy life.

We often overlook it as a tool because we say we don't have time to relax. But when we don't take the time we become more stressed, more angry and less capable of handling the daily problems with any form of constructive action. Relaxation can also be an important tool in managing our anger incidents.

Stress fuels our anger thoughts and turns them into anger situations. If we don't deal with stress on a daily basis, it can embroil us in more hostile moments than we ever thought possible. Following are suggestions for managing stress.

RESPOND TO YOUR BODY'S MESSAGES

When you feel tense . . .

1. Pay attention to your lower legs. Get off your feet and raise them to a resting position on a stool or chair. Relax the calves and release the tightness.

2. Next, focus on your back and spine. Get up and then release the tension by slowly breathing in and out. Relax and let go of the tension.

3. Practice breathing slowly. Feel your diaphragm and stomach contract. Do this until you feel relaxed.

4. You know how a tense neck feels. Roll your head slowly and shrug your shoulders afterward. Become aware of any tension and relax.

5. If your tension is strong, you may have a headache. Rest, close your eyes and think of pleasant, relaxing places.

6. Learn to focus on your muscles and practice relaxing them.

7. Go to a quiet place and meditate.

Activities That Help Us Relax

Sports

Dancing

Jogging

Walking

Laughing

Cycling

Sex

Massage

Imagery

Meditation

Ineffective Relaxation Methods

Overeating

Drinking alcoholic beverages

Using drugs

Withdrawal from other people

Ridiculing other people

Fighting

Sleeping

MORE ABOUT MUSCLE RELAXATION

The muscles become very tense when we are angry. Even the heart can get tense, so it is important to practice techniques of muscle relaxation. Here is a simple technique for relaxing:

1. Get into a comfortable position. Clench your fists until you feel the tension. Relax. Feel the freedom from tension when you relax. Repeat the procedure, noticing the tension and the release each time.

2. Now tense your biceps, feeling the tautness. Relax and straighten out your arms, feeling the release of tightness. Repeat.

3. Relax your entire body. (You may want to be lying on your back for this.) Just go limp and feel the weight of your arms and legs. Breathe in and out slowly a couple of times. Now hold your breath for a few seconds and notice the tension. Exhale and feel the freedom. Repeat by holding your stomach in and releasing. Do this with different parts of your body, paying close attention to the tension when you're restricted and the freedom when you relax.

IMAGERY

The technique of imagery takes us away mentally to the pleasant and relaxing places we picture. Breathing exercises are included for complete relaxation.

1. Imagine that you're resting on a white sand beach and the waves are rolling in and retreating. You feel the warmth of the sun and the peace surrounding you. All is quiet except for nature, the water, the breeze, the seagulls.

2. Inhale slowly and deeply, keeping your vision in mind. Allow your breath to be released with ease. Continue to feel the warmth of the sun and sand and repeat your breathing. Repeat and think positive thoughts you'd like at this time.

"I feel good."

"I like myself."

"I'm happy."

GETTING BACK IN CONTROL

Once again, practice closing your eyes and relaxing. Loosen any restrictive clothing and focus on your breathing. Once you feel relaxed, focus on the current anger problem. Visualize yourself in complete control and the exact way you want to handle yourself. Feel the confidence and don't forget to continue to breathe in and out slowly. Smile and say the words (the constructive words) you'd like to say to the other person. Picture the outcome you want. Now tell yourself you can handle any problem with confidence and without anger.

Visualization Exercise

It's now time to create your relaxing visualization. Go back and review the relaxation technique of your choice. From what you've learned, create your own visualization. Spend several minutes doing this and, in the space below, write down how you felt.

*Relaxing and visualizing made me feel . . .*_____

_____

_____

CREATING YOUR OWN IDEAL ENVIRONMENT

Once again, take several deep breaths and allow yourself to envision what you want.

1. In your ideal vision for your work, what does the environment look like? How would you like to handle work-related anger? How do you see yourself managing your problems?

_____

_____

_____

2. In your ideal home environment, how do you see yourself handling conflict or family problems? Describe how you'd like this environment to be.

_____

_____

_____

You cannot always control your physical environment, but you *can* create a mental environment that is pleasant and anger-free. Practice will help you get there before anger escalates.

THE DANGER ZONE

There are things you can tell yourself and things you can do to help yourself cope when you're in an anger situation—when you're approaching the danger zone of outbursts, hurt, abuse and outrage.

SELF-EVALUATION

You should now have a good idea of the thoughts that spark your anger. Let's look at some constructive thoughts that you can adopt to manage your anger. Put a check mark next to the thoughts below that you would like to use to replace your anger thoughts.

_____ When others disappoint me, it doesn't mean they don't like me.

_____ Each need is important.

_____ Adults can negotiate.

_____ I can want, but others can say no.

_____ Things aren't perfect and neither are people.

_____ People won't always do what I expect.

_____ Other people have different values from mine.

_____ I'm responsible for my own needs.

_____ Anger won't get me my way.

_____ Being assertive will help me express myself.

_____ People change when they want to, not when I want them to.

_____ We all have choices.

_____ Right and wrong is different for most.

_____ I'm not going to mind-read.

_____ Different things motivate different people.

_____ I'm not going to label this person.

_____ I'm going to take time-outs.

_____ Relaxing will help me cope.

_____ Conflict escalates anger.

_____ Negatives breed negatives.

_____ I will use neutral words.

_____ Attacks don't work.

_____ I'm not going to make a quick judgment.

_____ I won't be manipulated or manipulative.

_____ I'm going to learn to laugh.

_____ It's okay to make mistakes.

_____ I can manage anger.

Can you think of additional coping statements that you can use?

1. _____

2. _____

3. _____

4. _____

5. _____

Select a statement from the list that you can relate to most strongly. Write down why this would work for you and a situation you can relate to that it would help with.

_____

_____

_____

_____

_____

_____

_____

_____

_____

_____

WHAT DO YOU DO WHEN YOU'RE PROVOKED?

When we're confronted or attacked verbally, we start to feel the first signs of anger. This is the time to relax and focus on coping thoughts that will keep your anger from escalating.

Think of a coping statement you could use to . . .

1. Reassure yourself: _____

_____

_____

2. Stop anger thoughts: _____

_____

_____

3. Focus on the tasks: _____

_____

_____

When anger begins, pay close attention to your own voice and gestures in order to identify those habits that can lead to more internal anger and even a negative reaction from others.

Voice and Tone

1. Don't whine.

2. Don't yell.

3. Don't mock.

4. Don't mumble.

5. Don't snarl.

6. Don't sigh.

7. Don't groan.

Gestures and Expressions

1. Don't shake your finger.

2. Don't fold your arms.

3. Don't turn your back.

4. Don't pace.

5. Don't shake your fist.

6. Don't roll your eyes.

7. Don't sneer.

8. Don't shake your head.

9. Don't scowl.

10. Don't shrug.

11. Don't tap your foot.

So far you've learned how an escalating pattern of behavior can be prevented by:

- Using time-outs
- Relaxing
- Rethinking your anger thoughts
- Using coping techniques
- Recognizing habits that escalate anger.

You can also cope by using positive self-talk. You can learn to not only recognize present behavior that leads to anger situations, but you can also identify past behaviors and beliefs that trigger negative thoughts. We'll look at ways to get to the heart of this in the next section, but for now, take a moment to listen to yourself talk. Identify and write down some of your strongest emotions, your automatic thoughts and anything you'd like to say to yourself to rewrite your script.

My strongest emotions are: _____
_____
_____
_____

My automatic thoughts are: _____
_____
_____
_____

I'd like my new script to be: _____
_____
_____
_____

> "The blow of a whip raises a welt,
> but a blow of the tongue crushes bones."
> *Apocrypha, Ecclesiasticus*

SECTION

V

Letting Go of the Past

"The bare recollection of anger kindles anger."
Publilius Syrus, Moral Sayings

IDENTIFYING UNRESOLVED ANGER FROM THE PAST

Unresolved feelings from our past make us angry today, and they must be dealt with if we are to heal the wound. You have an opportunity now to discover what is really bothering you and to work out the anger you may have had for years. You must take the chip off your shoulder about the past in order to give up the pain and create a satisfying life for yourself.

Take the simple test below to help you recognize if you have past anger. Not everyone does, and not everyone knows whether they do.

1. I feel uncared for and unloved.

☐ Yes
☐ No

2. I feel sick with headaches and upset stomach.

☐ Yes
☐ No

3. I don't communicate well with my relatives.

☐ Yes
☐ No

4. I blame others for most of my problems.

☐ Yes
☐ No

5. I often want revenge when I'm hurt.

☐ Yes
☐ No

6. I'm never satisfied.

☐ Yes
☐ No

7. I just don't care to help others.

☐ Yes
☐ No

8. I go on binges of eating or drinking alcohol.

☐ Yes
☐ No

9. I don't seem to negotiate well.

☐ Yes
☐ No

10. I resent people who are successful.

☐ Yes
☐ No

If you said yes to most of the above statements, you carry anger and hurt with you every day of your life. You have many unresolved feelings to work out.

ACKNOWLEDGING THE PAST

For any behavior change, you must acknowledge the pain of the past and identify the situations that caused the hurt. It requires complete honesty with yourself and the desire to let go of the past.

Answer the following by completing the sentences.

1. I remember the hurt I felt when _____

   _____

   _____

   _____ and I'm still angry over that pain I felt.

2. It wasn't fair and I'd like to say that I don't deserve to feel this way. I want you to know that _____

   _____

   _____

   _____

3. When I think of this past anger or pain I want to _____

   _____

   _____

   _____

You can repeat this exercise for all the painful or hurtful memories you have of unresolved situations. Do this until you get out everything that is still a vivid feeling from your past. Express the feeling now! If you want to cry, do so. Think back to why you never expressed or resolved the emotion and how you would express it now.

Remember, it's okay to be angry with people you love or used to love and with those who love you. If you haven't expressed yourself because you didn't think it was right or you felt it was inappropriate, then you need to know that year after year your resentment has mounted, probably causing pain and hurt in your other relationships.

It is always helpful to have someone else help you work out these feelings. It is even helpful just to verbalize your feelings. It's a good idea to work with a clinical psychologist or other trained therapist. If you choose not to obtain counseling, then ask a close friend or relative to help. This should be someone who is not part of your past. This person's job is not to judge or give advice, but to listen and help you role-play your feelings.

The support will help you release built-up emotions and relieve the fear of expressing them or the shame of the guilt you may have for what you feel. It is always a good feeling to know that we are understood and listened to without judgment.

With your support person, find a quiet place where you will not be heard or disrupted. Face your support partner and breathe deeply, trying to relax as much as possible. Now picture your past anger situation and begin to describe your hurt and your feelings, just as you did in the written exercise.

Now think about the release of your feelings and feel the pain from the past slowly leave you. Imagine it is passing away, never to return. Continue to remember the situation and recall and describe how the other person felt. You may learn that both of you were hurt by the situation. You may feel silly doing this exercise, but you will feel better! It is also helpful to keep a journal in which you write down your present feelings and how they relate to the past.

One woman was having problems with her boss at work. Through writing in her journal, she finally realized that she was not angry with her boss, but with his manners, which were so much like her husband's. Her husband had never really praised her for her accomplishments and her boss also failed to do so. She finally told her husband how she felt and, through constructive writing, she chose the words to express to her boss her feelings about not getting recognized for a job well done. She let go of years of hurt by writing down her feelings first. She had the opportunity to take it one step further and confront her pain, but the writing could have worked by itself.

HEAR YOURSELF FEEL

If you don't like to write, you may want to express yourself on a tape recorder. It has the same benefits as writing, with the additional benefit of being able to hear the pain and hurt in your voice. This allows the emotion to surface. There is no threat here, and you can always erase the tape.

Remember that you are responsible for your pain. These are not exercises to establish fault or blame. You are the only one who really feels your hurt, and you're the only one who can change it.

We often feel good about our anger and believe that our past relationships are to blame for our unhappiness, and that our anger is well deserved. When we express anger from the past, we momentarily feel good because we are at that moment getting rid of anxiety. You may feel a sense of control when you express your anger or hurt—the control you never had over the situation in the past. This is an illusion, because in reality negative anger makes you less powerful and less effective in your relationships. You are simply acting out your contempt and a form of revenge.

If you're having difficulty identifying your past pain, it could be that you don't recognize it as pain or that you've suppressed it so long that it only surfaces when you have anger situations.

Reflect on these questions:

• Are you angry with your parents for anything?
• Are there past friends that disappointed or hurt you and you never quite got over it?
• Was there an authority figure in your life that hurt you or criticized you in an unconstructive way?
• Are you feeling guilty over things you said or did in the past?

A COMMUNICATION VISUALIZATION

Another way to let go is to take a short journey in your mind.

1. Close your eyes and imagine you are in a beautiful place, safe and warm and comfortable. It is in this place that you can let go and feel free. This place encompasses your life from the present to the day you were born. You have a good clear picture of your life.

2. Take a slow walk back five years. You are still in your safe and beautiful place—your forest or beach or land of enchantment. Are there people you know from five years ago that you want to say something to at this time? Select one person at a time and express yourself openly and honestly. Continue until you've communicated with everyone. Let them speak to you and listen carefully. Keep your eyes closed and feel the anger and pain leave you.

3. Go as far back as you would like in your life and repeat this exercise.

SELF-EVALUATION

Many of us have heard the little voice inside that affects our attitude and behavior. The sentences below may represent some of the things your voice has said to you. If you can identify with any of these, write down below each how it affected your behavior or fueled anger thoughts.

1. Our relationship would be better if only you understood me. _____

    _____

2. I won't tell you the truth because I'm afraid you won't like me. _____

    _____

3. If I act hurt, others will feel sorry for me and be nice to me. _____

    _____

4. I'd be successful if other people weren't so jealous of me. _____

    _____

5. I can't be what I really want to be, so I'll pretend I'm happy. _____

    _____

6. If I don't hope for much, I won't be hurt or disappointed. _____

    _____

7. I wouldn't feel this way if others would help me. _____

    _____

8. If you cared for me, you'd change. _____

    _____

9. If I'm sick or have a problem, I can get attention and love. _____

    _____

10. I can never do the things I enjoy because of all my responsibilities. _____

    _____

11. I'm not a lucky person. _____

12. Most people are out to get what they want; they really don't care. _____

    _____

Understanding the voice within can help you face reasons for disappointments, failed relationships and anger beliefs that may have been with you for many years.

EXPERIENCING ANGER FROM EXPECTATIONS

You can see that if you expect the worst, you'll probably get the worst. Your expectations can determine your behavior and your anger responses to others.

Even high expectations can result in disappointment and anger. When people don't do as you expect or don't come through for you, you may become angry, and both parties are hurt.

On the other hand, continually expecting someone to disappoint you will lead to anger before the other person even acts. Statements such as, ''You'll just do what you always do,'' can be anger-provoking for yourself and the other person.

High expectations of ourselves causes anger, because we become frustrated and disappointed in ourselves. We lose confidence and self-esteem when we fail to meet our own rigid standards.

Low expectations for yourself can cause you to become angry, because you'll give up easily and believe that you can't do things. Lack of confidence makes you feel bad about yourself and increases your chances of becoming angry.

When you identify your expectations, you can then decide if they are realistic. One way to test whether your expectations are realistic is to communicate them to other people; when they know what you expect of them, they have an opportunity to let you know if you are realistic.

KNOW YOUR OWN NEEDS

It is important for all of us to experience ourselves in a positive way, to feel good and to feel productive. We like to feel good about who we are. When we feel good, we act differently than we do when we are angry or feel unvalued. The cultivation of liking yourself is necessary for our well-being, our relationships and our job performance. Self-esteem declines when we do not communicate well, when we lack friends, when we don't feel accomplished or when we don't act on having our needs satisfied.

Anger can prevent you from maintaining a good, healthy level of high self-esteem. People feel best when the people around them validate their worth. When others support our self-esteem, we are more trusting, open and friendly.

Defensiveness is damaging for getting things done and building self-esteem. When people criticize, hurt, back-stab and start rumors, we feel hurt, angry and defensive. This leads to additional frustration and even loneliness.

TAKE TIME TO EXPLORE YOUR NEEDS

Listed below are basic needs; indicate how important each is to you by a checkmark in the best column. If you'd like, add your own needs.

Need	High	Medium	Low
Being liked			
Being popular			
Being loved			
Being creative			
Being challenged			
Being happy			
Being secure			
Sex			
Friendship			
Achievement			
Respect			
Peace			

SELF-ACCEPTANCE

Self-acceptance is the key to managing your anger.

It gives you choices. You see new choices when you accept any losses. You are free to move toward new goals and positive decisions.

It keeps you in touch. To take charge of your life you need to be in touch with who you are and like yourself for what you are.

It is becoming wiser. You learn from your mistakes, let go of the past and move forward.

It is freedom. Freedom to be the best at whatever you do, to have confidence, to go for it.

It is responsibility. You own up to what you are responsible for and accept responsibility for your own feelings.

NEGATIVE ANGER AS A MOTIVATOR

Anger can motivate, but we often pay a high price for such motivation. Why? Because . . .

- Negative emotions are intense, and this can damage all of our relationships.

- If you let your emotions drive you, there is a good chance you'll lose touch with reality.

- You make yourself vulnerable to other anger situations.

- You waste energy if the motivation works against you.

There are many more ways to motivate yourself. Anger should not be used as a motivator.

WHEN YOU FEEL BAD ABOUT YOURSELF

When you don't allow yourself to feel your anger thoughts, you can experience self-anger. The result is destructive, self-sabotaging behavior. You may get sick, look bad and become depressed. You end up not liking a thing about yourself.

We become angry at ourselves for many different reasons. For example:

- Because of things we do that we don't want to
- Because we weigh too much
- Because we don't start or finish a project
- For making a promise we can't or don't want to keep
- Because we said or did the wrong thing
- Because we made a mistake
- When we argue

BLAMING OURSELVES

We end up blaming ourselves for just about everything that isn't or doesn't feel right in our life. When we blame often enough, we suffer anger overload and we practice self-defeating, even destructive behavior.

If you don't know how to get in touch with your feelings or express them, there is a good chance you suffer from self-anger. There is usually a constructive strategy for dealing with self-provocation.

Example:

Self-Anger	*Strategy*
1. I'm angry because I don't want to always say yes to projects I don't want to do.	1. Learn to say no, and practice when you know this is not what you want.
2. I get angry when I binge and blow my diet.	2. Practice good eating habits and exercise. Join a support group for help.
3. I get angry when I let others yell at me.	3. Practice expressing how you feel and let them know you have feelings.
4. I get angry because I never have time to myself.	4. Make time and learn relaxation techniques.
5. I get angry because there are things I can't do.	5. Decide what you want to learn and go for it. Take courses in things that interest you.

> Using anger to change others or
> as a driving force is a no-win situation.

LEARN TO DIRECT YOUR THINKING

If you set goals for yourself and stick to them, you will find that you will become less angry. Chart your feelings, write down things you want to do and things you don't want to do, and channel your energy from self-anger and doubt into productive projects.

Learn to direct your thinking:

- Instead of getting angry at yourself for making a mistake, focus on what you need to do to make it right; get help if necessary and complete your project.

- Instead of getting angry at yourself for forgetting to do something, focus on doing it now or set up reminders so it won't happen again.

- Instead of getting angry at yourself for something you said, focus on making amends and practice skills for next time.

> The question to ask yourself is:
> *"What is my best choice for productive action at this time?"*

The faster you come up with productive action, the better your chance for cutting off the self-anger pattern. Do things that make you feel good about yourself. The happier you are with yourself, the less likely you are to feel angry with yourself for long periods of time.

SELF-EVALUATION

1. I get angry at myself when (or for) . . .

_____

_____

2. I can stop the anger by . . .

_____

_____

3. List at least two things you can do that are just for yourself in the next couple of days.

_____

_____

_____

BE GOOD TO YOURSELF

GIVE YOURSELF AFFIRMATIONS. Affirmations are positive thoughts we choose to say repeatedly to ourselves. It is known that affirmations can build confidence, stop negative beliefs and—yes—help prevent anger. Use affirmations to help manage your anger.

Here are some you may want to use. You can also create your own.

- I can change my life.
- I have learned from my experience.
- My past doesn't control my feelings.
- I'm a good person.
- I accept myself.
- I can do anything.
- I am worthy of love.
- It's okay if I make mistakes.
- I believe in people.
- I am loved.
- I enjoy what life offers.
- I can learn something new every day.

Write your own here:

My Affirmations

1. _____
2. _____
3. _____
4. _____
5. _____
6. _____
7. _____
8. _____
9. _____
10. _____

GIVE YOURSELF AFFIRMATIONS (Continued)

Now write down any affirmations you expressed but have a difficult time believing.

1. _____

2. _____

3. _____

4. _____

5. _____

Work on making the positive believable with your visualization techniques and go back over your new beliefs.

Examples: I am lovable.
I am good.
I am kind.
I am strong.
I am friendly.
I am patient.

Don't let past hurt and beliefs stop you from keeping your commitment to stop the anger thoughts. Remember:

• What we believe is what we create.

• We must clear limiting thoughts to make way for new beliefs.

• We must keep our vision clear.

Steps Toward Feeling Better About Anger

1. Observe yourself.

2. Be accountable.

3. Make a decision.

4. Be honest.

5. Develop a vision.

6. Acknowledge others.

7. Look for win/win situations.

8. Avoid blame.

REWARDS

Research shows that most people don't reward themselves for their successes. If you want to continue making progress, reward yourself when you recognize behavior changes and each time you take a positive step toward letting go of past anger or managing present anger.

Find time for at least a 15-minute reward and decide in advance what it is you'd like to do for yourself.

A reward must be just for you. It must relax you and provide you with pleasure.

In the space below, write down enjoyable ways you can reward yourself when you manage your anger thoughts.

1. _____
2. _____
3. _____
4. _____
5. _____

SECTION

VI

Listen to Other People's Anger

COPING WITH ANGRY PEOPLE

You've learned a great deal about kindling your own anger thoughts and behavior, but it is also important to know how to handle the anger that other people direct toward you.

Most of the techniques you have used on yourself will help with others, but you must remember that you are only responsible for dealing with your own feelings. You can avoid being manipulated by refusing to allow other people's behavior to make you feel bad.

Anger has a tendency to breed anger. If you express anger at an angry person, that person is likely to become even more hostile. If you have to deal with angry customers, employees, clients or relatives, there are four things you can do to manage the situation constructively:

1. Take the initiative and set the stage.

2. Find out what the underlying problem is.

3. Ask questions to find out what can be done to solve the problem.

4. Accept the other person's anger and look for appropriate ways to respond.

DON'T ARGUE

Don't try to persuade an angry person to change their feelings. First of all, they might be angry even without the problem. Even if their anger *is* directed at the problem, they are expressing it incorrectly. Instead of confronting the anger, deal with the problem.

AVOID CREATING MORE ANGER

Don't tell the angry person that they are angry or that they have no reason to be angry. Avoid using "anger words" yourself. Stay away from blaming.

AVOID BEING THE EXPERT

Statements that express that you know it all can only fuel the anger situation. Be careful of offering your opinion and the way you offer help.

COPING WITH ANGRY PEOPLE (Continued)

WATCH YOUR WORDS

Avoid "red flag" words when you are dealing with angry people. Here are examples of expressions that are likely to inflame an angry person further.

- You should . . .
- You're wrong . . .
- I demand . . .
- We can't . . .
- We won't . . .
- We never . . .
- You don't understand.
- That's stupid.
- You must be confused.
- I'm too busy for this.
- You have to . . .

Stop and think for a moment about what happens when some of these things are said to you when you're angry. Yet these are what we often say when we are confronted or attacked by upset customers.

Remember that people resent being judged and labeled negatively and being given no choice. These words and phrases result in lack of cooperation and motivation.

LISTEN, LISTEN, LISTEN

It is very important to first listen to what the angry person is saying before we comment, question or decide how to respond.

Guidelines for Listening:

1. Be attentive—as long as you are not being abused or battered personally.

2. Be interested in the other person's needs or problems.

3. Let the other person express himself without being judgmental.

4. Don't get hooked and jump into the anger.

5. Show you are listening with acknowledgment such as eye contact, head-nodding, etc.

6. Decide what action you need to take to resolve the conflict.

THE DIFFICULT PERSON

The difficult person we're talking about now is not the nuisance who may cross your path and vanish, but the person who really becomes a thorn in your side.

Most people faced with the unhappy task of dealing with difficult people try a rational approach. When this fails, they assume the individual wasn't listening, so they increase the volume of their voice or continue to repeat themselves. The difficult person usually feels nagged and refuses to cooperate.

First, you need to decide what *difficult* really means. If someone seems difficult to you because they don't do what you want or don't see things your way, then most of the difficulty lies in *you*, in your beliefs or expectations. If it's only one or two people you recognize a problem with and you're making considerable adjustments for their actions, they probably are difficult.

Suppose you have been covering up your co-worker's problems with a client. You have spoken to her about it many times and nothing changes. You must at some point let the person know that this cannot continue and that she needs to mend the client relationship or you'll have to stop covering for her.

It is important to note that often people who are continually difficult have problems of some kind. They may be frightened or insecure or stressed into chronic anger. They may respond to problems with anger and hostility, or even become tearful. In the case of insecure people, they often need feedback and reassurance. When they don't get it, they create problems so they can be told what needs to be done.

When the difficult person becomes belligerent, it is easy to get wrapped up in the emotion, but remember that anger breeds anger. You must sidestep the dramatic displays of emotion and focus on solving the problem. Keep your eye on the goal and don't fall into the trap of acting the way the difficult person expects. With the difficult customer, let them finish what they have to say, and then you can focus on the problem, not the anger.

86

THE DIFFICULT PERSON YOU MAY ONLY SEE ONCE

This could be someone you come across at the grocery store, on an airplane, when you go for service or when you're responsible for giving service. What you want to work on here is pure problem solving.

There are three basic steps to effective problem solving:

1. Define the Problem
This is usually done for you by the upset or difficult person.

2. Identify the Alternative Solution
Look for alternatives to arguing or escalating the anger.

3. Select the Right Solution
If your difficult person can't seem to express what they may really be upset about, select the solution that you feel will work best at this time.

KEEPING YOUR FOCUS

When you focus on the problem, you can start to cope, not explode. In every conflict your task is to communicate, to understand and to work out a solution. Following are statements that may help you keep your focus. Check the ones that will work best for you.

☐ I'll state my position calmly and simply.

☐ Try to understand the other person's position.

☐ Acknowledge the feelings being expressed.

☐ Ask the other party what will work for them in solving the conflict.

☐ Treat the other party with respect.

☐ Stick to the facts, not past beliefs.

☐ Negatives will not help the problem.

☐ What do I want from this?

☐ I won't blame.

☐ If at first I don't succeed, I'll try another strategy.

STAYING COOL

You need to keep your cool under fire, so that the other person's anger isn't fueled. Check the statements that would work for you.

- [ ] Getting angry will only make things worse.
- [ ] I'll stay calm; yelling has never helped.
- [ ] No attacking; this will only escalate the problem.
- [ ] This is a difficult situation, but I can work it out.
- [ ] It is time to cope. I don't want to blow my top.
- [ ] This will pass and I can handle it.
- [ ] I don't need to blame.
- [ ] I'm responsible for my feelings.
- [ ] I choose to stay in control.

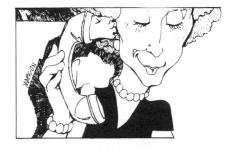

AFTER THE UGLINESS

It's important to calm yourself down after the conflict is over. Check the statements that would work for you:

- [ ] Forget about it. Think about something else.
- [ ] Get busy on a project.
- [ ] Do something for yourself that makes you happy.
- [ ] Reward yourself for keeping your cool.
- [ ] Relax.
- [ ] Call a friend; talk about good things and laugh.
- [ ] Don't take it personally or put yourself down in any manner.

In all your relationships, it is important to understand human behavior. Every person that we deal with is different. Each individual has his own likes and dislikes, his own personal set of ideas and values.

STYLES OF COMMUNICATION

There are four primary communication styles and, therefore, four types of behavior: expressive, amiable, driver, analytic. In practice:

- Most people use a blend of the four styles.

- Most people have a *primary* style and *back-up* style.

- Most people relate best to other people of the same style.

Each style has a unique way of expressing anger and a different level of tolerance for anger situations. Let's take a look at each style.

1. EXPRESSIVE STYLE

People with this style tend to be ambitious. They like to know what is going on and they take action to be involved. They react readily to influences, appeals or stimulation; they're emotional; they express their feelings and are very intense once angered.

Verbal/Nonverbal Characteristics

—Use their hands a great deal
—Wide range of voice inflection, fast-paced and loud
—Enthusiastic
—Disrupt things
—Speak before thinking
—Use emotional appeals

Shortcomings That Lead to Anger

—Lack follow-through
—Say too much
—Can overcommit
—Impulsive

Strengths in Dealing with Anger

—Sensitive
—Care for people
—Want things resolved

2. AMIABLE STYLE

People with this style tend to be easygoing. They like to be unimposing with others; they ask questions and listen; they react readily to influences; they are emotional and expressive with feelings.

Verbal/Nonverbal Characteristics

—Gesture inward toward body
—Soft voice, slow speech
—Smile
—Attentive
—Will go along with the crowd
—Concerned about what others think
—Low tolerance for chaos

Shortcomings That Lead to Anger

—Waste time
—Indecisive
—Not goal-oriented
—Feelings easily hurt
—Want to please too many people
—Won't express anger; only good

Strengths in Dealing with Anger

—Good listener
—Accepting
—Dislike conflict and want things resolved
—Will cooperate
—Doesn't have a temper

3. DRIVER STYLE

People operating in this style tend to be ambitious. They like to know what is going on and take action to find out. They talk a lot with others. They're self-sufficient and independent. They tend to be formal. They're controlled in the way they express feelings.

Verbal/Nonverbal Characteristics

—Use index finger to make a point
—Fast speech
—Finish other people's sentences
—Tend to be too serious
—Lean forward; territorial
—Easily bored
—Objective
—Very conscious of time
—Make quick decisions
—Seek to control

Shortcomings That Lead to Anger

—Need to be in charge
—Willing to confront others
—Aggressive behavior
—Strong-willed and forceful; critical
—Won't back down
—Hate to lose

Strengths in Dealing with Anger

—Goal-oriented for conclusion
—Determined and disciplined

STYLES OF COMMUNICATION (Continued)

4. ANALYTIC STYLE

People with this style tend to be easygoing. They like to be unimposing with others. They ask questions and listen. They're self-sufficient and independent of others. They tend to be formal, controlled and cautious with feelings.

Verbal/Nonverbal Characteristics

—Gestures tend to be controlled
—Monotone speech; slow rate of speed
—Tend to ask detailed questions
—Walk is slow and plodding
—Show little enthusiasm
—Preoccupied
—Ponder; difficulty making decisions
—Concerned with facts and figures
—Low tolerance for chaos

Strengths in Dealing with Anger

—Thorough with the facts
—Cautious; won't say anything they don't want to
—Persistent; willing to work on the problem

Shortcomings That Lead to Anger

—Perfectionism and little patience for mistakes by other people
—Stubborn; want to be right
—Indecisive; frustration because of the inability to act quickly
—Aloof; problems with relationships and openness

TIPS FOR CONFRONTING THE DIFFERENT STYLES

If you keep the other person's communication style in mind, you can interact with them more successfully.

Expressive Remember that they make decisions quickly and easily, and they will be motivated by incentives, recognition and attention.

Amiable They don't like making decisions that may put them in a bad light with others, and during conflict will need lots of stroking. They want to be a part of the solution and to be liked.

Driver They will be clear and decisive because they know what they want. This person needs to be involved in the solution to the conflict.

Analytic They collect masses of data and will only end a conflict once they feel the right decision has been found. Motivating factors for this person include being given facts, having details and allowing them to act in an individualistic manner.

YOUR FAMILY RELATIONSHIPS

A loving, positive relationship is the result of clear, open communication. Because relationships need mutual understanding and support to grow, the relationship usually falters when communication efforts fail.

Anger festers when it is not openly dealt with, and shaming, hurt and blaming often result. This can lead to hostility and destructive behavior.

Anger created by *avoiding* contact with family members is usually far more damaging than the conflict that started the problem. One of the biggest mistakes we make in our loving relationships is bringing up past experiences. Things your partner said or did that hurt you or offended you:

- "You had to get drunk at the neighbor's party."
- "I remember how you flirted at my brother's wedding."
- "You wouldn't fix it when I asked; now look at what's happened."

Statements such as these build anger and resentment that can be repeated throughout the entire relationship. They create distance and may even end the relationship.

If someone in your family has caused you pain in the past, either forget it or express your feelings once and for all. You can also express the hurt to yourself, work through it as you learned in previous exercises, or verbalize the hurt to the family member who hurt you.

It isn't easy to work out negative feelings, but you can do it without creating any additional anger situations. Here are some suggestions:

1. Don't blow the incident out of proportion. If you recall it only when that family member makes you angry, there is a good chance it isn't very significant.

2. Focus on the good in the relationship and forget the little nagging items.

3. When you recall the incident, ask yourself if you played a role in escalating the problem. Remember—be honest!

4. If you must bring up the incident to stop dwelling on it, do it only once; express your feelings without blame and tell the other person your expectations.

5. Ask yourself if the other person actually intended to hurt you.

6. Ask what could possibly be gained by holding onto the resentment.

Now think of any incident about which you hold resentment with a family member. Choose only a parent, spouse or one child at this time.

HONESTY QUESTION

Do you express past-hurt anger to your partner?   Yes ___ No ___

---

20 ADDITIONAL BEHAVIORS THAT CREATE RELATIONSHIP ANGER

1. The Need to Be Right

The need to always be right and prove it can cause many angry moments in relationships. This is often acted out by someone who has to demonstrate superiority or it can be based on a simple insecurity and desire for approval. Either way, it can create adversaries instead of partners. It is one of the main reasons family members bicker.

Partner #1: "I told you about that."
Partner #2: "No, you never did."
Partner #1: "I did. You weren't listening."

In some cases, the issue can be far more serious than the above exchange. It can create lasting resentment and additional communication problems for weeks and even months to come.

HONESTY QUESTION

Do you need to be right too often?   Yes ___ No ___

---

2. Negative Criticism

We can grow from positive, constructive criticism. We can learn from comments that are helpful. But it is very easy to criticize, in a negative way, our family for their mistakes, habits, beliefs and everyday behavior.

We are often not aware of how hurtful we are, and it becomes a habit to blurt out negative comments.

- "You did it wrong again. You'll never get it right."
- "You just aren't any good at that sort of work."
- "You say the stupidest things when you get around other people."

Statements like these don't lead to any positive change and cause hurt, anger and self-esteem problems. Constructive requests or comments would be better and less hurtful.

HONESTY QUESTION

Do you criticize your family in a negative way without even thinking about what you're saying?   Yes ___ No ___

---

3. Passing Judgment

You will not always approve of what your family members do, but chronic disapproval and judging can damage any relationship. It is also unrealistic to approve of everything all the time.

Request a change of habit in a constructive way, and discuss the changes and the reasons without destructive impact.

Negative: "I don't like the way you always yell at the children."
Positive: "Could we discuss a way of correcting the children without yelling?"

HONESTY QUESTION

Are you consistently evaluating and disapproving of
your family's actions and behavior?   Yes ___ No ___

---

4. Threats

Threatening is a sure way to escalate an anger situation in any relationship, and families find this very insulting. The threat of causing pain to someone you love is aggressive and hurtful, and it's not easily forgotten.

Threats linger on long after the heat of the argument is over. They are rarely made in a calm, rational tone and they offer little value in resolving the conflict.

- "I won't take this. I'll take the children and leave."
- "Do that again and you'll never get another dime from me."
- "Your mother would love to know how you're acting. I think I'll call her."
- "Wait until your father gets home."

You can state your feelings without any underlying or blatant threat. Expression is assertive and reasonable; threats are not.

HONESTY QUESTION

Do you often threaten in a family argument?   Yes ___ No ___

---

20 BEHAVIORS (Continued)

5. Emotional Outbursts

Negative drama makes your family members feel helpless, manipulated and drained. Outbursts can be frightening and they escalate anger thoughts. Tearful pleading and drama create a breakdown in total communication. Expression of feelings (even negative ones) is healthy, but there is nothing beneficial about negative dramatics.

Stop yourself and think of what you're doing. If necessary, take a time-out and come back to the discussion at a later time.

Those with a temper should be cautious in any anger situation and practice relaxation techniques on a regular basis.

HONESTY QUESTION

Do you display negative dramatic behavior when in conflict with your relatives?   Yes ___ No ___

---

6. Interrogating

Questions, questions, questions—they can be exhausting. They tell your partner or family member that you don't trust them or believe them, or that you must control them. This can be destructive to any relationship and create anger moments that will escalate into full-blown arguments. No one likes to be cross-examined. You don't like it done to you, so be aware of when you do it to loved ones.

Show respect for the privacy of family members. Just because they are your family doesn't mean that you have to know everything they do.

Wrong Choice: "Where were you?"
Better Choice: "Are you okay? Did you get hung up at the office?"

This may take practice, especially if you are the suspicious type. But with a little effort, you'll find it produces more open communication with your spouse and children.

HONESTY QUESTION

Do you interrogate partner or children?   Yes ___ No ___

---

7. Labeling

We discussed labeling as part of our belief system, but now we're talking about the psychological terms you use against your partner or even your children. This is probably in the top ten of all offenses that we commit in relationships.

- "You're so stupid."
- "You need help; you're crazy."
- "You're nothing but a child."
- "It's not my fault you're insecure. I can't help you."
- "Stop asking so many questions; you're paranoid."

Using negative labels like these can only hurt the people you love and create anger that will be stored up for another incident. Sometimes the labels are even more aggressive with complete evaluations attached to the label.

"You're abnormal. No one acts the way you do. It's probably due to your fear of rejection."

Don't play psychologist with your mate or child. It will not help the situation.

HONESTY QUESTION

Are you aware of labeling members of your family?   Yes ____ No ____

---

8. Indifference

There probably aren't too many of us who haven't experienced indifference in a relationship. We can and often do take partners or family members for granted. We get used to their presence and we can even lose interest in what they say or do. This damages relationships at the time of the incident, but it can also drive your family to seek attention and communication elsewhere.

We are being inattentive when we don't respond verbally, walk away when the other party is talking, ignore something of importance or change the subject when the other person is still talking.

Attentiveness is important to any loving relationship and to a happy social life.

HONESTY QUESTION

Do you often ignore family members when
they are seeking your attention?   Yes ____ No ____

---

20 BEHAVIORS (Continued)

9. Lying

Lying in a loving relationship weakens even the strongest ties. It undermines the trust and respect the two of you should maintain. It is better to say nothing than to lie. "I'd prefer not to talk about it" is far better than an out-and-out lie. If you get in the habit of telling lies to avoid conflict, the relationship will be even more damaged than if you face the consequences of your actions.

Be aware of when you lie and why. Out of love and respect for your relationship, make a commitment to never lie.

HONESTY QUESTION

Do you lie to your partner or family members to avoid
conflict or the consequences for your actions?   Yes ___   No ___

SELF-EVALUATION

Before we go any further, take a moment to assess what you've learned about yourself and your intimate relationships. Please complete the sentence below. Express any thoughts you have that could help you have greater satisfaction in your current relationship.

I've discovered that I could have better family relationships if I . . . _____

_____

10. Jealousy

Jealousy is a negative emotion that contains its own set of anger thoughts. This anger is usually the result of insecurity, the fear of loss and possessiveness. Jealousy is usually a reaction to beliefs and perceived harm rather than factual information. But, perceived or real, creating an emotional scene or displaying anger will not do any good for your relationship.

If you react emotionally instead of rationally, you are certain to damage an already shaky relationship. Learn to trust, and work on building your own self-esteem. If your suspicions prove to be real, you must then decide about the future of the involvement you have with your partner.

HONESTY QUESTION

Are you jealous without cause?   Yes ___   No ___

11. Using Negative Language

Negative emotional language can be hurtful and cause anger resentment. When you express yourself emotionally in a positive situation, you enhance your relationships, but negative language can cause long-term damage.

Describing your feelings without dramatic display is your best choice in any anger incident.

Negative emotional language can be very damaging to your children.

A statement like "Your father just left and walked out on us" can inflict emotional scars that last for years. Be careful of your language in an anger situation with a family member. The effort will be well worth it for those you love.

HONESTY QUESTION

Do you use negative emotional language with
or about your family?   Yes ___ No ___

---

12. Complaining

We often use relationships to air complaints about life. It seems to be a safe avenue for venting our feelings about work, emotions in general or just world events. Complaining can cause your partner to feel guilty about not siding with you or to feel sorry for you when they can't or don't know how to help. This can build resentment and anger if it turns into habit or even a way to manipulate.

It is true that we can't always report the good about our day, but you can discuss events without the anger that accompanies complaints.

The entire tone of your evening can be set by the way you communicate your feelings.

1. State the situation as it happened, good or bad.
2. Request advice or assistance from your partner with a problem.
3. Remember: your partner didn't participate or create your problem.

HONESTY QUESTION

Do you complain too much, too often?   Yes ___ No ___

---

20 BEHAVIORS (Continued)

13. Pessimistic Outlook

We can easily destroy the enthusiasm of others with a pessimistic outlook. Without thinking, we may put down ideas or hope when they are expressed by our family members.

- "I don't know why you planted those seeds. They'll never grow."
- "Why have you started that project? You know you'll never finish."
- "That won't work."
- "It'll just rain."

Have you heard statements such as these? If you have, you know how harmful they can be to your relationship. Negative people can become very angry and often have some past anger that has not been worked out.

HONESTY QUESTION

Are you a pessimist?   Yes ___ No ___

---

14. Comparisons

Comparing your loved ones to others in an unfavorable way is sure to fuel anger situations.

- "You're just like your father."
- "You never see Jim talk to *his* wife like this."
- "Why can't you be more like your brother?"

This type of statement is particularly destructive when anger situations have already been started over another negative behavior. Remember that no one is perfect, and comparing will not change the behavior or solve the problem.

HONESTY QUESTION

Do you compare your family members to others
or in an unfavorable way?   Yes ___ No ___

---

15. Blaming

Blaming never benefits anyone. Here's a blaming statement: "I shouldn't have listened to you. It's your fault we're lost." This is just as harmful as blaming yourself. Remember that you're responsible for your own feelings and your own actions. When you blame your family for things that are your responsibility, you are really looking for a scapegoat.

16. Attacking

Attacking is unpleasant under any conditions. When you attack things that others say or do, you are attacking their sense of self-esteem. Most people will stay away from the source of an attack. This is a sure way to drive your family members away and shut down communication.

HONESTY QUESTION

Do you attack members of your family?   Yes ___ No ___

17. Mind-Reading

We all try to mind-read with our partners and family at one time or another—we make interpretations about family members' thinking without asking them what *they* think is going on. This creates problems in relationships.

Do you really know what someone else is thinking? Don't guess. You'll save many angry moments by asking a few questions before you assume anything.

HONESTY QUESTION

Do you mind-read?   Yes ___ No ___

18. Giving Commands

Sometimes we forget to ask our family members to do something. Barking out orders is difficult for anyone to live with for long.

- "Get the door."
- "Pick up your clothes."
- "Don't do that."
- "Shut up."

They can get worse when we go into detail.

- "I told you never to act that way in front of my friends."
- "How many times do I have to tell you to shut the gate?"

A request works much better. A simple "please" and "thank you" can go a long way.

HONESTY QUESTION

Do you give orders instead of make requests?   Yes ___ No ___

20 BEHAVIORS (Continued)

19. Pretending

Pretending to like something or to be happy, or pretending you're not upset when you are doesn't help to build a solid relationship. The truth usually comes out sooner or later. Be honest without being cruel. You'll save yourself frustration and resentment down the road.

HONESTY QUESTION

Do you pretend in order to avoid problems?　　　　　Yes ___　No ___

---

20. Punishing

When we punish our family because they haven't lived up to our expectations, we are breaking down the lines of constructive communication. Rather than discussing the problem and looking for a solution, we punish by refusing to do something, by sulking or even by causing such guilt that our partner can't enjoy the day. Find a solution that works for both of you.

HONESTY QUESTION

Do you punish when you talk?　　　　　Yes ___　No ___

Relationships take work. Family relationships are sensitive to all behaviors that are anger-provoking. Destructive habits can easily be corrected if both you and you partner make an effort. Stop and think before you act. Be aware of the message you are sending and what you are doing. You and your family will be happier and healthier for the effort.

TEACHING YOUR CHILD TO MANAGE ANGER

Children who are not taught to manage anger are prone to many problems such as drug abuse, lying, stealing, fighting, depression and poor health. You can work with your child to express emotions in a positive way. Discuss their hurt and help them understand that there are boundaries to work within. Here are six suggestions for helping your child learn to manage his or her anger.

1. Positive reinforcement is a powerful tool that you can provide for your child.

- Praise encourages cooperation.
- Reward for good behavior builds self-esteem.

2. Know why your child is angry.

- Communicate and be in tune with your child.
- Teach him or her to express feelings.
- Be a good example.

3. Explain consequences for negative behavior and positive behavior.

- Don't threaten. Explain the choices or options.
- Teach your child the facts.
- Help your child solve his or her own problems.

4. Spend time with your child.

- Ask what they want to talk about.
- Ask opinions on family matters.
- Don't criticize your child for expressing feelings.

5. Communicate your expectations and make sure your child understands them.

- Be realistic; after all, you are dealing with a child.
- Don't yell. Explain what is expected and why.
- Ask your child what he or she thought the situation was.

Remember that if you teach your child through positive example, you will instill values and behaviors that can last a lifetime. All of the techniques for dealing with your own anger situations can be applied when you train your children to manage anger. Be consistent. Children expect their parents to act a certain way, and when you respond differently to conflict each time it occurs, it can create confusion and additional anger for your child.

SELF-EVALUATION

1. Do you ask your children how they are feeling? _____

2. Do you know the things that provoke your children? List the things you know of and the strategy you can use to help them in their anger situations.

My Child's Provocations

1. _____
2. _____
3. _____
4. _____
5. _____

Problem-Solving Strategy for Provocation

1. _____
2. _____
3. _____
4. _____
5. _____

3. List some things you can do to help your child communicate and express feelings in a positive way.

_____

_____

4. What are some consequences of behavior that you can explain to your children?

_____

_____

5. How can you help your children set goals for positive self-esteem?

_____

_____

6. Express honestly any feelings you have about your current relationships with your children.

_____

_____

ANGER AND YOUR WORKING RELATIONSHIPS

Whether you are the boss or the employee, anger on the job is not acceptable when it is handled inappropriately. The inability to handle anger on the job can lead to a whole list of consequences—all bad. These can include termination, early retirement, being passed up for a promotion, reduced productivity and a poor working climate. Some job provocations to be aware of are:

- **Deadlines.** Pressure to have a project completed when there is little time can create stress, and stress can lead to anger situations.

- **Criticism.** Anger can occur when you've worked hard but face what you feel to be unjust criticism.

- **Passed over.** When you don't get the promotion you've worked hard for and felt you deserved, you may find yourself angry.

- **Incompetence.** When you count on your employees or co-workers to do a good job and they don't, you are likely to be upset.

- **Rumors.** Being the victim of false rumors or jealousy is a common source of anger around the workplace.

- **Overworked.** Having too much to do or being given duties that are over your head can cause frustration and anger.

Don't let job frustration lead to aggression. Aggression is a striking out in an attempt to destroy a source of frustration. It can also be a sign of inner fear, and it can take on many forms. Some people use gossip and ridicule instead of physical violence. As they make others look foolish, weak or inadequate, they feel "bigger" by comparison. Here are tips for coping successfully with job stresses.

TIPS FOR COPING

1. Make your own goals and decide that you want to keep your job.
2. Make an effort to be friendly.
3. Communicate constructively with your boss, employees and co-workers.
4. Demonstrate your willingness to find a solution.
5. Assess the situation before you act.
6. Practice time-outs.
7. Consider the consequences of negative behavior.
8. Remember: you're part of a team.
9. Stop the anger escalation with relaxation.
10. Be responsible for your feelings.

ANGER AND DEFENSIVENESS

We can improve on-the-job relationships when we become sensitive to a person's defensiveness and turn it into cooperation. Suggestions:

- Recognize defensiveness for what it is. Do not become defensive yourself.

- When possible, reduce the threat; offer approval and respect.

- Create an atmosphere of open communication and understanding.

EFFECTIVE LEADERSHIP CAN REDUCE ORGANIZATIONAL ANGER

If you are a manager or leader, your style makes a difference to the people around you. Effective leadership sets a climate for productive and happy employees.

Organizations can slide into having an angry climate if there are persistent problems in the workplace. Problems that can lead to group anger include:

1. Lack of supervision

2. Managers that play favorites

3. No recognition

4. Overworked

5. Little or no communication

6. Misuse of authority

7. Managers won't listen

8. No training

9. No goals

10. Poor planning

When employees perceive that the organization is more important than they are and that their needs are not seen as important, they become demotivated and angry. If their needs are integrated with the needs of the organization, they will be more productive and so will the company.

PREVENTATIVE TECHNIQUES FOR YOUR COMPANY

Here are some simple preventative techniques that you can adopt in your company:

Analyze your own attitude.

Take a genuine interest in others. Take an active role in their suggestions and be aware of their needs. Have confidence in your employees and show it by word and action.

Have group discussions.

Communicate with employees. Explain company objectives and goals. Explain why each goal is important and how team effort can work. Let them know the purpose and importance of their job and how each project fits in with the corporate mission.

Encourage participation.

Ask others for their opinions and ideas. Employees enjoy being supportive and playing a role in achieving an objective.

Keep it stimulating.

When employees become bored and lose the sense of challenge, they focus on the negative. Employees like the responsibility of meeting a challenge; it requires initiative and develops self-reliance and pride.

Promote team spirit.

Team effort builds rapport, team pride and camaraderie. People with a common purpose will unite and get along better.

Be approachable.

Open communication helps individuals to vent problems without fear. This eliminates frustration and hidden hostility.

Administer discipline fairly and impartially.

Inconsistency triggers employee discontent. Help manage organizational anger by handling complaints promptly and by listening for details and facts.

PREVENTIVE TECHNIQUES FOR YOUR COMPANY (Continued)

Give Recognition.

You can boost morale when employees know their hard work will be appreciated and recognized. Remember that people work for more than just a paycheck.

Be thorough.

Explain rules, policies and expectations. Clear communication of expectations eliminates problems before they begin. Hold update sessions and ask questions to assure common goals and mutual agreement.

S E C T I O N

VII

Review

INTEGRATING WHAT YOU'VE LEARNED

The exercises you've done in this book are just the first steps for managing the anger in your life. By now you should have a sense of how to be happier. You should also have the desire to eliminate the pain of anger.

You've learned that whatever you focus your attention on will be what drives you to present the behavior of your choice.

You've seen that not changing destructive behavior can cause more pain and anger than changing it, and that new ideas and behavior can bring you better relationships and inner peace.

When we learn new things, it's easy to slide back into old behavior. Here are some suggestions for staying on track in managing your anger:

• Know what causes your anger.

• Decide to change the feeling before it escalates.

• Try new approaches until one works for you.

• Visualize the behavior you want to prevent.

• Discover how to handle the situation better.

• Be consistent in your positive behavior.

RECOGNIZE YOUR BELIEFS AND VALUES

In order to change your anger thoughts, you must know what beliefs cause your provocations. You need to discover a new belief that will change the way you feel when you're angry. Your thoughts and actions are going to create the end result. If your actions are positive, your results and life will go in a positive direction.

Be Ready for Change

You cannot learn to manage your anger unless you're willing to let go of old behaviors and adapt new ones. Here are the best ways to change:

• Believe that the anger must change.
• Practice techniques of change.
• Learn to relax.
• Take time-outs.
• Condition yourself for new behavior.
• Think about your outcome. Visualize a triumph, feel it and link it to the rewards you'll receive.

INTEGRATE WHAT YOU'VE LEARNED
(Continued)

Body and Mind

You need a healthy physical body as well as healthy emotions. Remember that your body responds to the strain of anger and stress in a negative way. You can improve your health if you:

• Focus on a healthy body.
• Visualize the healthy body you want.
• Practice techniques to relieve stress and good conditioning.
• Ask yourself questions about what you want to accomplish.

Manage Your Attitude

Your attitude determines your behavior and the end result of your anger situation. Remember that you are responsible for your own feelings and actions. Here are things to watch yourself on:

• Beware of your communication style.
• Practice your breathing.
• Watch your facial expressions.
• Check the tone of your voice and select your words carefully.
• Change your anger into energy.
• Be assertive, not aggressive.

Let Go of the Past

You cannot let go of your anger without letting go of the past. Remember to:

• Let go of the conflict of the past.
• Change negative beliefs.
• Know your own values.
• Recognize that other people have different values and beliefs.
• Know your rules and choose whether to change them.
• Know the pain of your past and then forget it.
• Identify new pleasures for letting go of old anger.

Goals

Since anger is often related to unrealistic expectations and frustrated goals, it is important to deal with goals constructively:

• Identify your purpose and set goals.
• Be realistic and know your expectations.
• Don't create needless pressure and anger frustration with unattainable goals.
• Make your goals work for you; don't just work at your goals.

Habits

Your habits help shape your emotions. Negative habits can harm relationships at work and with your family. Be prepared to admit and change bad habits. Create new habits with a new script, and practice them repeatedly until they are as familiar as the old destructive habits.

Be Positive

Know what makes you feel good and use these things to create a positive state of mind. Here are some useful techniques:

- Visualize your positive outcome.
- Let go of pessimistic beliefs.
- Choose your emotional state.
- Reward yourself.
- Identify negative tendencies to sabotage yourself.
- Feel good because you want to.

Now Go for it!

Decide what you want and how you want to feel. Develop your change strategy. Take constructive action. Be flexible. Be happy!

DON'T GET ANGRY—
GET HAPPY!

AND GOOD LUCK!

NOTES

NOTES

NOTES

NOTES

NOTES

NOTES

NOTES

NOTES

OVER 150 BOOKS AND 35 VIDEOS AVAILABLE IN THE 50-MINUTE SERIES

We hope you enjoyed this book. If so, we have good news for you. This title is part of the best-selling *50-MINUTE™ Series* of books. All *Series* books are similar in size and identical in price. Many are supported with training videos.

To order *50-MINUTE* Books and Videos or request a free catalog, contact your local distributor or Crisp Publications, Inc., 1200 Hamilton Court, Menlo Park, CA 94025. Our toll-free number is (800) 442-7477.

50-Minute Series Books and Videos Subject Areas...

Management
Training
Human Resources
Customer Service and Sales Training
Communications
Small Business and Financial Planning
Creativity
Personal Development
Wellness
Adult Literacy and Learning
Career, Retirement and Life Planning

Other titles available from Crisp Publications in these categories

Crisp Computer Series
The Crisp Small Business & Entrepreneurship Series
Quick Read Series
Management
Personal Development
Retirement Planning